A SHEEPDOG
NAMED OSCAR

A SHEEPDOG
NAMED OSCAR

Love and Companionship in Rural Ireland

DARA WALDRON

**SIMON &
SCHUSTER**

London · New York · Amsterdam/Antwerp · Sydney/Melbourne · Toronto · New Delhi

First published in the United States of America by DoppelHouse Press, 2025
This revised edition published in Great Britain by Simon & Schuster UK Ltd, 2026

1 3 5 7 9 10 8 6 4 2

Simon & Schuster UK Ltd
1st Floor
222 Gray's Inn Road
London WC1X 8HB

www.simonandschuster.co.uk
www.simonandschuster.com.au
www.simonandschuster.co.in

Simon & Schuster Australia, Sydney
Simon & Schuster India, New Delhi

The authorised representative in the EEA is Simon & Schuster Netherlands BV,
Herculesplein 96, 3584 AA Utrecht, Netherlands. info@simonandschuster.nl

A CIP catalogue record for this book is available from the British Library

Trade Paperback ISBN: 978-1-3985-6230-1
eBook ISBN: 978-1-3985-6231-8

Typeset in Bembo by M Rules

Printed and Bound in the UK using 100% Renewable Electricity at CPI Group (UK) Ltd

MIX
Paper | Supporting
responsible forestry
FSC
www.fsc.org   FSC® C013604

For Anton

Why that gloom, son of Oscian?
What shades thy mighty soul?

— James Macpherson

Dilige, et quod vis fac.
Love, and do what you will.

— St Augustine

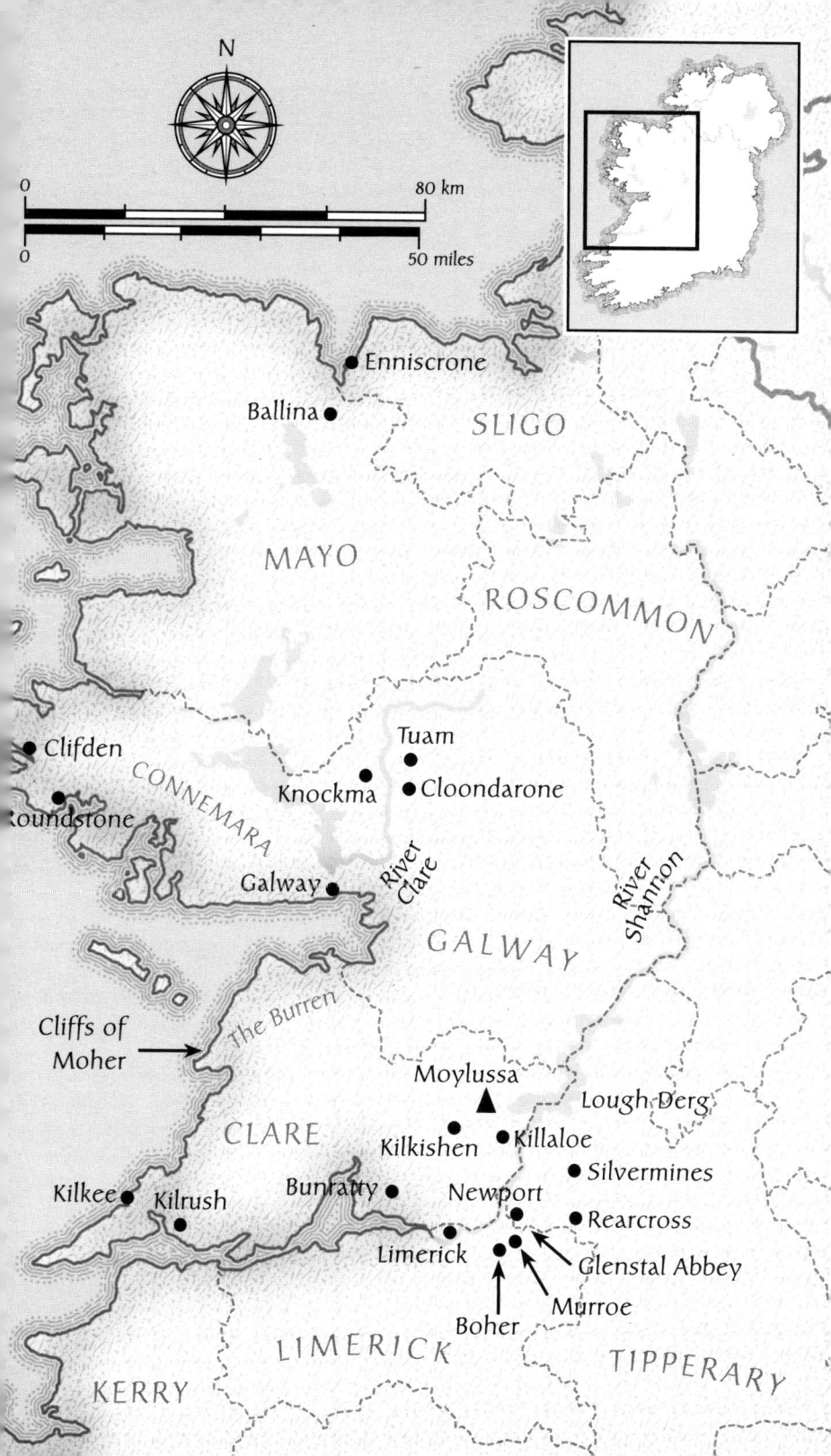

CONTENTS

1

The Rescue Act

The weekend habits of my toddler son had begun to so-
lidify. During breakfast, Anton would turn and utter the
words '*Finding Nemo*'. Tired and sometimes half-asleep, I'd
slip the tape into our VHS machine. We'd sit back together
and watch the film from beginning to end. At some point, I
estimated we'd seen that picture more than a hundred times.
It was difficult to countenance a child's need to watch the
same thing over and over to a point of banality. But he did.
We both did.

Some years later, a critique captured my attention: it's a film
about separation anxiety. Nemo is a clownfish with a disfig-
ured fin, a young male who is captured from the wild and
placed in a fish tank. Dory, a female of another species who
suffers from ongoing memory issues, nonetheless helps Nemo's
father, Marlin, to look for him. Nemo eventually escapes
and is reunited with his dad. Perhaps Anton was experienc-
ing something like Nemo? In this stage of development, he

was exploring and asserting his independence. By repeatedly watching the movie with me at his side, he was learning to cope with the prospect of being on his own.

This story is also about being alone and counteracting it. It, too, is a story about inter-species companionship, love and loss. A sheepdog named Oscar became my companion. He came into my life on the first anniversary of the death of my father, John Waldron. Somehow, I believed that Oscar found a way to me. Our lives intersected at a time when he was a stray in need of a home, and I was astray and in need of a friend, one who didn't ask questions when doubts and uncertainty swirled around in my head.

My family lineage is a typically Irish one. Both my parents worked as GPs and left Ireland for Manchester in the 1970s to work in a British hospital. They returned to County Galway to take over my grandfather's practice soon after I was born (my grandfather Tony Waldron was a GP for Tuam Sugar Factory, a public-owned and run sugar and beet factory in operation from 1934 to 1987).

My father was a complex character, not easy to put in a box. He was something of a contrarian, enjoying the to-and-fro of debate and happy to play devil's advocate. He was seemingly contradictory in that he identified as a Labour voter long before the Labour Party propelled Ireland's first female president, Mary Robinson, to victory in 1990 (a day which my mother Mary and her friends celebrated with panache), while maintaining the exclusive position of hunt master with the North Galway Hunt throughout the '80s, an expensive role at a time of real poverty in Ireland. As a doctor, he was an idealist, helping to found the Galway Planning Clinic in the late '70s, dedicated to the 'progressive' cause of making contraception legal while helping mothers to manage their family demands at a time when the economy was in a precarious state. Some of my earliest memories of being with him are car journeys from Tuam to Galway, from a town in the north of the county to 'the Clinic' in the city. I would often wait hours for him to finish his evening session. Sometimes, I would wander up Shop Street to O'Briens newsagents and browse the magazines. But at other times, agitated and bored, I walked the streets, counting to myself, waiting for my father to proclaim 'I'm finished, let's go'.

Weeks after he died, I was contacted by researchers who were working on the history of family planning in Ireland. We talked about legality and illegality, about Mary Robinson and about my father's role. Our conversation offered some justification for my memory: their research presented Ireland as a conservative country, dominated by the Catholic Church. Though it was economically poor back then, it was rich in culture. Music, poetry and literature seeped out of every corner and crevice, and on several occasions my father helped us partake in it. He took me and my older sister Sheila (Sheila was born in Ireland in 1972, before my parents left for England, while my younger sister Kate was also born there in 1982, after their return) to the first stadium concerts in Slane and Croke Park. When Bruce Springsteen played Slane Castle in 1985, on the back of the anthemic 'Born in the U.S.A.', my father's excitement in taking his children to see The Boss, a figure who had immortalised blue-collar struggle on the margins of life, was palpable. The same year, I remember cheering at Bono and U2 on their return to Dublin for the 'A Sort of Homecoming' show (with a young, brash REM, a late addition to the line-up), my father scooping 12-year-old me up onto his shoulders. Bono wrapped himself in the tricolour as 'Pride' rang around the stadium and I remember feeling loved. I idolised – beyond words, really – this man who had lifted me onto his shoulders to see the stage, as the stadium transformed into one huge mass of energy.

In this regard, my father helped instigate change, which was coming to Ireland at this time, accelerated not so much by the decline of the Church, but the influence of the world beyond: Britain, Europe, the US. It was the world that U2 had begun to conquer and the youth of Ireland were awakening to. My father loved his time in the UK in the '70s and came to embrace its modern ways, yet he was all too aware of the tensions brought by change. He was an avowed atheist but signed off on my attending a Catholic monastery boarding school, Cistercian College Roscrea, at the age of fourteen. He was in a battle of ideas with the Church, but it never stopped him from supporting a school that offered education based on values he shared: loyalty, bravery, chivalry and hard work.

Shortly before he died, I sat with my father in a country church for the requiem mass of a lifelong friend. As we waited for the funeral to begin, I mentioned my surprise at such a well-attended service, given the rumour that the deceased was also an avowed atheist. 'He wasn't much of a believer,' my father said, 'but he wasn't taking any chances.' We laughed. My father's declaration about another encapsulated all that was complex about himself: his suspicion of the old ways married to a guarded respect for their longevity. It is no surprise, given this unusual combination of 'progressive' and 'conservative' to use the terminology of our day, that his children – myself and my two sisters – would come to inherit many of these same traits.

I was also fourteen when our family purchased a small farm on the outskirts of Tuam in a place called Cloondarone. A few years after the land in Cloondarone was purchased, my father built a house and stables on the land with a view to breeding thoroughbred racehorses: living the dream. Ireland's horse breeding industry was largely situated in the more arable midlands, or in the east of the country, but my father's dream was to make the west a serious competitor. He was a lifelong lover of horses and the culture that was associated with National Hunt racing in Ireland. Already well known locally, he achieved a wider degree of respect in later life as the breeder of Faugheen, one of the country's most revered racehorses, nicknamed 'The Machine'. His adored mare, Miss Pickering, passed away with sepsis after foaling a half-sister to Faugheen in June 2016. My father, sleep-deprived from the days leading up to Miss Pickering's death and still grieving her loss, scoured the country for a foster mother. He eventually found one in Fethard in south Tipperary, a big piebald mare who took on the task.

A few days later, tired and fatigued, Dad was killed driving from a point-to-point, an amateur National Hunt race meet in Ballingarry, County Tipperary. He was involved in an accident and died instantly. He suffered little to no pain, I told myself. He was doing the two things he loved: acting as medical officer for a horse event.

In later years, but before the meteoric rise of Faugheen intensified his obsession with racing, I would often drive up to visit Dad in Cloondarone. Shifting planes of landscape, twisting roads and the swift move from green to bog signalled that I was no longer in Ireland's midwest – the part of the country that I now call home – but once again in the hue and cry of the rural west, into which I was thrust as a teenager and where the rhythm and pace of life seemed a little slower – and where a giant hare was rumoured to move elegantly through the back field of my father's estate in Cloondarone.

As I turned the sharp left towards his living quarters, and the stone walls built during the Famine years crowded me in, a small sheepdog peeked out from behind a hedge. Gabriel Lardner's dog was in pursuit of the moving object otherwise known as my car. It was a signal.

In the months after Dad's death, I regularly travelled to Cloondarone to stay in the house he built beside the stud in the mid-'90s, my parents having separated when I was eighteen. Sometimes I looked at the big foster mare in the brazen fields, the foal sucking on her teat, and thought of my father's desire to keep that foal alive. I often walked his land back then. Staring at the line of horizon from an elevated position, the land seemed to hold some deep recess of mystery into which I yearned to be thrown.

One day, I walked down towards the River Clare, across small mounds that seemed like miniature versions of the drumlins that are found further west, the fields that led towards the river a light shade of green. Within a certain distance of the riverbank, the landscape dramatically changes. There are no trees, no shrubbery or growth – just a smooth area of grass that seems to have given up on embellishing its space. As I peered over at the river, a twig was sticking out from the side of the bank, like a small tree that had designs on much greater things but lacked the support to get there. Then I suddenly became awash with involuntary memory, thrown deep – just as Marcel Proust famously experienced when nibbling a madeleine – into an event that I think shaped my father's later life without him ever being fully conscious of it. It's an event that sheds light on his character: his bravery and his challenges as a father.

It was a Sunday in October 1983. As usual, he was with the North Galway Hunt. I was nine years of age and was out all morning kicking a ball with neighbourhood friends. From what I heard later, the mood was jovial as the hunt waded through the River Clare, the horses and riders in sync, their feet fading into the murky shadows. A thick brown stream signalled the seasonal turn. Another signal was the thundering flow, the grip of the current that causes white foam to congregate on its surface. The steep banks made large sections of the river difficult to cross. The hunt followed a scent that necessitated crossing through the river and had planned to go over at a shallow section. But in October, as winter beckoned, the river was deceptive, the draw of the current much greater than it might have seemed. The group moved through the water slowly. Nobody felt that the shallow level was any significant danger. But one of the hunt members, John Croke – a family acquaintance at the time – began to slip from his horse. Perhaps more frightened than he was letting on, given he was unable to swim, he suddenly became tangled in the reins. As he struggled to free himself from his riding equipment, he was caught by the current. What seemed at first like fun and games soon turned to disaster, as John was pulled away by the river. My father, a strong swimmer of competitive standard in his youth, dived in and grabbed hold of John. He demonstrated incredible bravery in risking his own life attempting to save another and managed to drag his friend to the bank, where my father snatched hold of a twig. But it was not enough to prevent the current from whisking John from his grasp.

Not privy to the tragedy unfolding in real time, I remember getting home and ringing the bell of the front door. The side gate must have been shut, so I was unable to get in the back. Above, the musky autumn grey was a damp imprint of humid skies. Someone let me in and I made my way upstairs. The bathroom door was ajar and I glanced in. The image of my father in the bath with his back to me and his head in his hands hit me with significant force. It was like a reverse shot, a film image that cuts from a frontal view to a view from behind instantaneously, that signals the story ending. I heard only of what happened from others later, never from the source. I knew nothing of my father's restless nights, the guilt of his survival; that knowing that some adjustment in the river, some sleight of hand, might have made all the difference; that a family was changed for ever in that instant; that one could hold life and death in your hands and not know it; that death would win. My father received a national award for bravery, which was reported in the Irish daily newspapers. But none of it meant anything to him.

Years later, when I gazed across the river, searching for the little path that led from the bottom field, I thought of that event again. Like a lot of Irish men who were brought up to believe that displays of emotion were a sign of weakness, my father struggled with his emotions. He found it hard to go back there, to relay the events that had taken the life of another father, to feel the sadness and dejection that he undoubtedly felt. Like his own father, who never spoke about the Irish Civil War that pulled the country apart, Dad never spoke about the day he jumped into the river to save a drowning man.

For all the struggle in speaking about his emotions, my father had that great ability to chat, always putting strangers at ease. He loved a swashbuckle entrance into the pub, hailing those sat at the bar like he had just entered heaven. He adored the occasion of the end of week when the Irish put their ailments and troubles aside. The town bursts into life and, for a moment, nobody cares if you are king or pauper. A local 'doc' who caressed and disdained notoriety, he embraced the publicness and everyone-in-it-together possibilities of the Irish pub. Those Friday night entrances into the Rustics Vaults in Tuam, when my father would order pints at the bar before settling in to wait for others to arrive, hold a special place in my heart. They are shards of time that form a big part of a crystal.

I loved him, but our relationship was strained in the months before he died. I knew that he had watched his own father die a slow painful death and that it haunted him. Like W. B. Yeats, the poet laureate of the west of Ireland, he found getting older to be a distressing experience. As he aged, he became less tolerant. His feet began to give him problems and he had a small toe removed. I have a vivid recollection of him trudging through the streets of Manchester on my fortieth birthday as he tried to hide his pain. Ageing was enemy number one because he didn't want to live in his head; to feel the body breaking down like a car that is losing its warranty.

When he passed, in the difficult times that followed, I told myself he was doing what he always did. By all accounts, he had been in good spirits. He died on a Sunday and his body was brought to the University Hospital in Limerick and then to Tuam. The funeral arrangements were the first thing put in place. He was waked on a Tuesday, followed by a Wednesday evening 'removal', when he was laid out in a local funeral home so that the general public could pay their respects. On Thursday, having been removed to the church, the funeral mass was held, followed by a meal. It was, and still is, custom in Ireland to have a meal for those who travel. There were 200 seats at my father's meal.

In an Irish wake, a grieving family member or a friend stays with the body throughout the night and day. I can still recall the sadness and pride felt in equal measure when listening to my first cousin Sarah Lowry sing 'Sonny' – a song written by Ron Hynes and sung by the Irish chanteuse Mary Black – to her father, my uncle Vincent, as he was laid out before her. The song speaks of a loneliness felt in the long hours of the night, one that must have resonated as she sat with his body in the dark hours that followed – the lyrics confirming that she was alone, yet contradicted by the force of all our presence with her.

The attendees of the wake rally around the grieving family, dropping meals to the door in some sort of jubilation for the life lived. Celebrating the dead person's portal into the next world is designed to cover over, to suppress, the void that will eventually open. My father was gregarious and popular, and his wake was a full-thronged affair in the summer, a vast collection of friends and family. Afterwards, admirers marched through the halls of the funeral home, as is traditional in Ireland, for nearly five hours. My hands felt blistered that night from shaking hands.

In the weeks that followed the week-long funeral proceedings, I entered something akin to a dream state, compelled by the duties of a son to oversee the various obligations needed to sort out an estate. Numbed from the loss, my body was pent up with get-it-done adrenaline. He died without a will, which meant a level of stress that exceeded the usual chaos.

Sudden death precedes strange and complicated grief. Numbness, anger, eruptions of sadness – the parameters normally accredited to life get jumbled up. The lyrics to a song that once uplifted become signs of the dead, an absence nestling within as the ghost of time. The five infamous stages of grief are hard to find parity with, as the relationship with the dead lives on in new and undefined ways – in the culture that transcends the individual but seems to speak for them. There is an exhilaration and a customary need to take control, to shape the mourning into something the dead would approve of, as if they are still there in some form, watching over the proceedings.

Sudden death is also a springboard for denial, for that deep feeling of disconnect from knowing, designed to suppress the impression of loss needed to pass through the intense pain. And one of the more malignant effects of grief concerning sudden death is in the difficulty of processing it as real. Years after the death, those left behind still expect the dead to wander in the door, just as before.

Months after his funeral, I sat with Ylva, my wife, in a pub outside Limerick city. I was nursing a pint of Guinness when the ghost of my father stumbled in the door, rubbing his hands together with glee. Then he wandered up to the bar as I watched his spectre move like a ballerina on stage. He turned around and held the railing of the bar with his small hands before looking me in the eye. 'This is where you've been,' he declared for everyone in the bar to hear, as I smiled, blushing back with pride. I thought that, by conjuring the ghost of my father, I would triumph over my grief; that if I could summon him back and use all the resources of the imagination bestowed upon me, I could pass through the halls of sorrow. But, as I found out, it is much more complicated than that. It isn't linear and it comes in waves. There is no point where you can say 'It's over'. One cycle begins and another ends. Life is a river we are all trying to cross on horseback. But the unexpected current keeps us from doing so in the way we originally planned.

Grief was at its most intense when the noise of daily life was turned down, when friends and colleagues assumed the worst had passed. Shock wore thin. Christmas 2016 was when the real loss began in earnest. Although I'm not especially traditional a person and am no fan of ceremony, the symbolic nature of Christmas, when families rally together from all around the globe, brought the loss home like nothing before. I sat at my computer on Christmas Eve playing the song 'Waves' from Kanye West's album *The Life of Pablo* on repeat, sipping on oversized measures of whiskey. The song, featuring the rapper Kid Cudi, addresses the lack of sunlight on our wellbeing, akin to a bird's inability to fly in a cage, and the feelings that stay with us when someone leaves. That year I had developed a strange affinity with the song's deeper sentiment, identifying the trauma of loss as a theme underpinning the album. The sublime beauty of 'Waves' was undeniable, a reckoning with grief akin to waves that roll in. Some waves are predictable, but others could turn tidal.

It was almost a year after my father's death that I met Oscar. In the spring of 2017, as a distraction from the oncoming anniversary, I phoned a friend to let him know I was on the lookout for a new dog. Loe McDonagh, a settled Irish traveller, had kept horses and greyhounds on my father's land for many years. He had stepped up to the mark after Dad died, overseeing the everyday running of the farm.

I phoned him on a May afternoon to talk about our new home in a rural village called Murroe, which we had purchased on the back of the turmoil the previous June. Having witnessed Loe's care of animals firsthand, I knew him to be an animal lover. I trusted his judgement. Our conversation was short and to the point.

'Hi Loe.'

'Well, Dara.'

'Listen. I want to ask you something.'

'Yea. Go on.'

'I'm getting a dog.'

'Okay.'

'I'm wondering what dog to get. You've seen where we live when you dropped down the table.'

'Are you beside a farm?'

'Yea. Near a village. There's a dairy farm across from us.'

'Is it fenced off?'

'I suppose it is. There's just a big field behind us.'

'Get a sheepdog, Dara. Border collie. They're loyal, they herd. A terrier could chase sheep or cattle and be shot.'

'A working sheepdog?'

'A retired one. Yea.'

'Where will I get one of those?'

'I'll have a look out for one if you want.'

'Ah. Good.'

A sheepdog, a working dog – the type so often seen in rural Ireland tied to a shed by a rope, the kind that pops up on the old TV series *One Man and His Dog*, running at the beck of a farmer's call. A border collie? I rarely used the name. Where did the name come from? Which border was it referring to? Anything that referenced a border carried negative connotations during the Troubles in Ireland.

My thoughts then focused on the abject associations with the word 'sheepdog' when growing up in Ireland. Back then, sheepdogs were markers of paralysis, of a family stuck in time.

They signified an unhealthy attachment to the past. They were an impediment to the future. A new world was forming in towns like Tuam as part of the newly emerging post-industrial age, while sheepdogs were signs of an agricultural past with an unwanted influence on the present. Staring up from a crouched position, they roamed outside, ready to work at the sound of a farmer's whistle. They stared up with beady eyes, consumed by boundless reservoirs of energy.

Following our initial conversation, I collected more information. I began to undertake research into sheepdogs and collies online and across various media. Border collies were usually, if not always, working dogs: herders. For Irish farmers, a working dog herds sheep and cattle. If it fails to display a required instinct or intelligence, it does not really matter how it's referred to. A sheepdog is foremost known for its ability to work. One can source a collie from a breeder, I grasped, but if it fails to display a herding instinct, it might not even be called a 'sheepdog'. It seemed to me that the terms were really messy, the distinctions between them – so important to rural traditions – incredibly hazy.

I was keen to follow Loe's advice, which meant that I wanted to find some kind of sheepdog, a border collie, whatever that had meant. But I had no idea where to look. I was about to type 'retired border collie/sheepdog' into search engines and social media sites when something serendipitous occurred: the real moment of discovery. In my job as a university lecturer, I regularly meet with students on a one-on-one basis. One afternoon in a tutorial with an MA student called Anne Stewart – and with the issue of dog rescue at the forefront of my mind – I took the liberty of interrupting the conversation to ask Anne if she happened to be a dog owner. Originally from Northern Ireland, Anne was living in Kilkishen, a small village in East Clare and had been resident in the vicinity for thirty years. Although forced to move south during the Troubles at the age of thirteen, she was still very Northern in her affections. Her eyes lit up when she heard the word 'sheepdog'.

She had seven dogs: six were Maltese terriers, one a border collie. Anne described how the pack grew to this number over time. Her son, Michael, a successful fashion designer, chose the terriers for their luxurious coat and Anne didn't have the heart to sell off all the puppies when they bred. Jake, her trusted collie, was an outside dog and more of a loner than the rest of her pack. I mentioned our family's move close to the border between Limerick and Tipperary, and that I wanted to adopt a retiree sheepdog from somewhere.

Anne sat back in her chair. Everything seemed to slow down as I waited for her next words with bated breath. I was intensely aware of my surroundings. The light shone in through the window beside my desk and there was something meditative and settling in sitting in a room lit by natural light, especially when winter in Ireland offered so little. May is the month of optimism, when the hope that the rain that spilled down in record amounts would stave off for a few days and the full dint of summer appears. Evenings stretch — 'there's a stretch in the day' is the most commonly heard phrase — and spirits rise. Rays of sun pushed through the window that afternoon, as dust particles drifted in the air like granules of a new and coming time.

'That's kind of crazy,' Anne returned in a Northern brogue, her dimples pushing against a steely smile. 'There's a wee sheepdog alone on a farm down the road from me. A beautiful thing.'

The wheels of chance began clicking into gear, luck pressing down from some undefined source. It seemed like a ridiculous proposition.

'Nobody owns him?' crept tentatively from my lips.

'No,' Anne replied with some care. 'He strayed to the village and then returned to the farm alone. He's from a farm for sure as he has no collar and stays in a shed.'

I took some time to dwell on her description. 'You mean a stray sheepdog is living there? Who feeds him? Who looks after him by day?'

Anne shifted in her chair, a movement that brought with it a certain unease about the sheepdog's origins. Her tone changed, secreting an air of Northern suspicion. It was a disposition I would gain a greater understanding of as the year progressed. She was anxious in her deliberation, sighing and pushing her hair out of her eyes.

Then, turning her gaze upon me she declared, 'Collies are two-a-penny, Dara. If the warden gets him, he'll put him down. There are so many across the country. Smart and beautiful animals. The problem is that nobody wants them.'

'Nobody wants them' was commensurate with the impression formed in my childhood, that sheepdogs are remnants of a past to break free from. A picture took focus in my mind of a father returning from work with a black-and-white puppy under his arm, a gift from a local farmer. I imagined

17

his children reacting with disdain. *Not a sheepdog, not a farm dog. Look at how it moves.* The children wanted a Labrador or a King Charles; a border collie was too common an Irish dog. To come upon the breed in any shape or form was to reject the future. And, in the west of Ireland, the future was all we had to cling to.

At my desk that afternoon, as the word 'collie' was mentioned again and again, something began to stir. I would kick against the pricks, step out of my inertia. It was mere days since I had spoken to Loe and now Anne was telling me of a sheepdog that made its way into her life – and possibly mine. A mix of excitement and fear washed over me, but it was followed in the aftermath by an urge to ditch the plan for an easier dog.

Why the angst? Why the hesitancy? I had been, of course, forewarned about the energy levels of collies. I was concerned that the dog would be in my face day in, day out. I was grieving and didn't need a hyperactive dog in my life. I sat back, listening, before committing to go to see the dog, offering nothing more definite for the time being. I was non-committal for other reasons: the first anniversary of my father's death lay on the calendar horizon and I lacked the mental and physical fortitude to adopt a dog in the interim weeks.

The term 'rescue dog' also frightened me; rescue seemed to involve care and attention I wasn't capable of offering. What would happen if the dog was mentally scarred from neglect? What would happen if the dog had developed behavioural issues because of the same? Surely I wouldn't be able to adopt if that was the case? But I had a stubborn streak. I had put myself in a certain position by asking Anne about dogs and something made me want to follow through. I would make the visit. I knew I had to do it – for myself, as much as anything. At worst, I would get to spend some time in the countryside, having lived far too long in the suburbs. And, perhaps, beyond these concerns, things would be okay.

Anne sent me a picture that weekend: a digital photograph of a dog staring out from a decrepit shed. It was difficult to read anything definitive into the photograph, other than that the dog had the good sense to find a quiet corner and just stay there. Apparently, the neighbours had taken to feeding him in the evening, yet he still didn't wander down towards their house as a result. He just stayed put. The person he encountered most – apart from the neighbours – was the old farmer's nephew, who was working on the land by day, having been left the farm by his uncle when he went into a home with dementia.

It was an intriguing photograph, in that it suggested intelligence and instinct: intelligence to hide in a shed and instinct to find a quiet space on a farm. But there was still much the image did not reveal – most of all, a personality. Huddling together around a smartphone, enlarging and minimising the photograph, my wife and I attempted to elicit some meaning from it. The more we looked at the image, concocting a narrative of before and after, the more frustrating the gaps in our knowledge became. There were so many questions. How big is he? How dirty? All that was visible in the picture was a head nudging through a doorway. How feral is he? He sleeps outside in a shed. Is he aggressive? Was he beaten? Is he damaged?

Anne was heading off for a few days and, having received the photo on Saturday, it wasn't possible for me to visit the dog – whom Anne had named Oscar – until Wednesday. In the meantime, I read up about the difference between buying a dog and adopting, and how adopting had become the new norm. I had not bought a pet in years and so much had changed since my teenage days; so many more animals had become unwanted as consumerism had entered the scene. As a result, thousands of dogs – once the thrill had passed – were put up for grabs. I began to research animal rescue and the culture around it. In legal terms, dog ownership had changed so much in such a short space of time, with activists believing it was a moral duty to rescue dogs from abusive owners. Some believed it unethical to breed dogs in a world where so many are discarded. But there is still a cost attached to rescuing; many animal lovers give a portion of salary to shelters to keep up their good work, while activists give generously to shelters through both finance and voluntary service, donating food and offering to walk the dogs if needed.

Niall Harbison, who is Irish, has become something of an online sensation in his quest to save as many Thai street dogs as possible, with celebrity fans such as Liam Gallagher adopting from his Happy Doggo sanctuary in Thailand. Harbison's dedication to the street dogs he rescues and nurtures back to near or full health is unwavering; as a result, his story has inspired a huge number of people to get involved in dog rehabilitation and rescue activities. Some of the cases documented on his social media feeds tell such vivid stories. The one I found most intriguing, and pertinent to my own potential rescue, was about a husky named Bowie, found in Thailand underweight and undernourished. The juxtaposition of the breed and landscape – huskies are typically associated with the Nordic regions, not the dry soil that is such a feature of tropical regions in South East Asia – captured my attention immediately. Huskies were bred to pull sleds through the snow-covered expanses of the north; Thailand was known for humid sticky streets and vast exotic beaches drenched in sun.

Bowie's story chimed with Oscar's tale in one sense at least: Oscar seemed heavily wedded to the farm surroundings I was, perhaps, about to displace him from. Removing a sheepdog from territory they are so bound to is, I learned, one of the challenges rescuers face with such intelligent and incredibly sensitive breeds. I understood working dogs were particular castes of animal, so the process of adapting him to an alien environment frightened me. The rescue bug had yet to fully infect me like it had Harbison, but, nonetheless, even with this concern around things needing to be in their right place, when I pictured Oscar peering out of that shed, like the light penetrating darkness, a warmth in me grew, driven by some renewed belief in life itself: that goodness can shine through in any setting.

The culture of dog rescue and its focused care has evolved in tandem with an animal rights movement I had some knowledge of from my university years. Animal rights, I understood, are inextricably linked to morals concerning sentient life. Do animals feel emotions and pain like humans? If the answer is yes, then to hurt a dog is not so different from abusing a human and so some kind of intervention is needed to reintegrate an injured animal into the folds of regular life. Harbison has openly linked his urge to rescue to his recovery from his self-destructive addictive tendencies. His personal story is evidence of the transformative moral purpose around the human urge to rescue fellow animal beings.

The dog peeking out from inside a farmhouse shed – the subject of the photograph Anne sent – had a certain mystique in this regard. The act of peering out from a doorway was near human as an affectation; there was a gentle configuration to the face of the animal clinging to the security of his shed. Beside Oscar was an empty agricultural feed bag, along with the frame of an old bed: traces of a forgotten century, signifiers of the past. The animal feed was emblematic of farm life, the bed a family heirloom. What became, I thought, of the people once attached to these things?

No amount of staring, however, could instil enough confidence to think I had the nurturing capabilities to help a traumatised dog. No amount of speculation could account for a lack of experience, that gnawing feeling that I wasn't – we weren't – ready to care for the dog. I told Anne I was having second thoughts, that my commitment to the idea was waning. In her melodic Belfast whistle, she set me at ease. 'He's a lovely wee thing, Dara, wait and see,' she said, shoring my confidence enough to allay my creeping concerns.

There were still several days to pass. Keeping busy helped quell the doubts I harboured about taking the dog home, work keeping my general unease at bay. On the day I was due to travel out to Kilkishen to finally meet Oscar, the sun burst through the clouds. A long winter had given way to a tentative spring and was finally offering a blushful summer, manifesting in one of those impenetrably hot days that makes Ireland such a unique place. Moods brighten, people drink in public and playgrounds fill up; the people – like flowers – bloom instantaneously. It was one of those sun-drenched summer evenings that seemed designed for lounging about in the countryside, a time to be outside on an island so often marked by belligerent weather and rain that powers in from an unruly Atlantic.

We decided that my then 13-year-old son Anton would accompany me and that we would report back to Karl, our younger son, and my wife Ylva when we got home. The plan was simply to see the dog, to assess whether he was suitable to adopt. The visit to the farm was a kind of recce to determine the state of affairs. And so we ate our dinner together hastily as the conversation turned to collective excitement. Our thoughts were entirely taken up by the prospect of our visit to the farm. Then Anton and I were off, the planning and speculating turning to action.

The idea was to travel the motorway between Limerick and Clare before hitting the country road. An intense sun shone down and wind pushed through a half-open window, a cacophony of sound whistling through the air. I searched around for music to quell the lull in adolescent–father relations. Bob Dylan's *Blood on the Tracks* (a favourite) jumped up. 'Tangled Up in Blue' began ringing out as the car lurched forward into an Atlantic headwind. Taking the straightest route to the farm brought with it a clear goal: to see this dog and, if things went well, to bring him home in a few days.

It felt good. Life was simple for a change. We had a clarity of purpose.

The single byroad to Kilkishen required a left turn from the motorway, taken in the direction of Sixmilebridge, which signalled a change in landscape. A dusty back road replaced the concrete of the earlier route. Twists and turns released shadows caused by the overhanging greenery, while bustles of green growth drooped over the front of the ditches like curls on the forehead of a dishevelled youth. Anne had planned to meet us in the large village of Sixmilebridge, the idea being that we would follow her car along another back road to the farmyard where Oscar had made his home. She messaged me to say she was running late, so we retreated to the riverside to drink a Coke and listen to the draw of the river drifting past. A wild, near-romantic mysteriousness seemed to rise from the ever-changing colour of the water as it trickled down, blue morphing into twisted variations of green and silver.

There are so many delights to this region of County Clare. Moylussa is the highest peak and is best approached from Twomilegate, a lakeside retreat on the outskirts of Killaloe. It offers a majestic, relatively short hike with panoramic views of Lough Derg, one of Ireland's largest, most beautiful lakes, and over to Sixmilebridge and Kilkishen. On weekends, hikers and mountain bikers spend time climbing and cycling the trail and its multiple pathways. The final part of the hike is a little steep, passing a mountain road onto a trail that involves some passage through rocky terrain. Some newly embedded tracks allow hikers to move along wooden planks that shield them from the boggy earth. From the summit on a sunny day, the view of the lake gives witness to its full glory. The region is scattered with smaller lakes like the one to be found outside Kilkishen, where we were heading.

Folklore and myth also play a big role in this part of Clare. It is a region of the island marked by pagan and early Christian lore. Infamous sightings of the banshee, a mythical Irish faerie woman, are recorded in this area. The most notorious account comes from the memoirs of Lady Fanshawe in 1665, when she was staying in the region. Lady Fanshawe was awakened by a scream, after which she looked out her window to find a woman with a dishevelled and unkempt mane of red hair. Sometimes seen combing her hair, the banshee tells of an impending death. The banshee seen by Lady Fanshawe was thought to be the ghost of a peasant wife of a former owner of the abode. Sure enough, the morning after the sighting, Lady Fanshawe heard of a family member's sudden death. While accounts vary in detail, the banshee, of which there have been several sightings over the centuries, is a typical 'faerie' in this region. Lady Wilde, the folklorist and mother of the poet Oscar, has drawn attention to the small size of the banshee as indicative of her faerie status. The apparition foreshadows death, but the cry of the banshee is also said to be the most piercing and distressing sound known to humans.

Time and myth are knitted into this landscape of wells, ringforts, castles, mountains and lakes. The former high king of Ireland, Brian Boru, was born near Killaloe and one of his brothers worked as a bishop there. Holy Island on Lough Derg, where relics of early Christian Ireland are preserved and meditative retreats are held year-round, is one of the most interesting places to visit. From the Cromwellian invasion of the seventeenth century to the Catholic Emancipation movement of the nineteenth, history erupts from a landscape removed from the otherworldly veneer of the western seaboard. Hills and musky lakes contrast with an austere sea-beaten landscape known as the Burren (gushing in summer) in the west of the county. As you approach Kilkishen, an arrow of time inches you forward; the driver is suspended in a terrain of rusting signs and church spires reaching to the sky. It's like you're breathing in and out of the past.

Having met Anne, we followed her car along a byroad, passing a playpark and fields of grazing cattle on a steep incline, at which point a smaller byroad unfolded before us. It was like a vision of the time when horses and traps were the only source of transport across the island, back to the decades past when the first experiments in communism were taking place in the Ralahine area, long before communism came to fruition elsewhere. The commune of Ralahine, founded near Newmarket-on-Fergus in 1831, formed in resistance to colonial-religious hierarchy, an inspiration for the Ralahine Centre for Utopian Studies at the University of Limerick, of which I am an affiliate member. The centre took inspiration from the legacy of the East Clare commune, with its radical attempts to reshape Irish society at the time. It is a research group influenced by the original East Clare initiative.

Anne's car pulled in on a slight bend in the road. We had arrived at her cottage, a small and cute residence with a shed and partly manicured garden. I stepped from the car to a sudden influx of colour. In the valley below, a small turlough

27

glistened against a radiant sky. From the roadside cottage, the spectacular view made itself known, like a lost Bruegel masterpiece. Symmetrical hills shouldered Clonlea Lake, a picturesque inland lake upon which there were several small fishing boats. To the right of this was a steeper incline, the fields peppered with buttercups and medium-sized bushes of gorse, while sheep and newly born lambs decorated the green expanse of hills. A two-storey house, beside which was a farm, was further down the road from Anne's cottage. From there, a path led up to the farm where Oscar had taken refuge.

'Nice here,' I said, restless but keen at the same time. 'Where is Oscar camped?'

Adjusting her rimmed spectacles, Anne pointed at the hills across from us. The farm could be approached from two directions, she announced, a frontward-looking gap in the wall where visitors entered and a back route requiring a short trek up a steep hill.

With a collar and lead in my pocket on the off chance he was difficult to approach, we made for the back entrance, trekking up a trail that would lead to the shed Oscar made his home. The terrain was hilly enough to make it difficult for Anne to traverse, so we decided to change route to one of the less sharply inclined steps of land before calling in on a neighbour – a veterinary nurse called Laura who was feeding Oscar – to say hello and then trek along the man-made path back to the entrance of the farm.

It is difficult – but not impossible – to describe the breathtaking scenery at the top of the hill on entering the walled garden where Oscar was waiting. The shed, as shown in the photograph that Anne had sent on, was hidden in this space. We passed through an inlet, over cowpats and through the gate of the stunning eighteenth-century walled garden. With a curved design so unlike the strict lines popular today, the space exuded its own resolute beauty.

'He's in here,' Anne said to me, with some trepidation. She very much wanted me to take him home.

But I was getting ready to back-pedal, to fashion a way out of taking the dog. Once firmly inside the farm, on the cobblestone path that lay beneath a shaky red gate, it felt like we had broken free of the present, settling in a different time. There was something entirely magical about the quasi-symmetrical curvature of stone around, the space where animals could move freely within the enclosure. There was no trace of a flower bed, just weeds, as if a garden had been neglected for decades. To the right of the enclosure, just visible through the gate, was the stately home marked by a caved-in roof. It was, Anne said, a listed building protected by the state. The house was falling apart, but the brickwork around the house, in the sheds, was born of ancient longevity: the timeless serenity of stone.

There were different-sized sheds additional to the one in which Oscar had made his home and a larger farm area with finely executed stonework perpendicular to this. At the point where the end of one building could conceivably have met the other was a gate, through which I could ascertain that the farm sat in the shadow of the 12 O'Clock Hills as they are known today: a routed set of walks through the sumptuous landscape of East Clare. In the midst of these hills is the

Sunyata Buddhist Centre, an unsurprising location given the meditative quiet one experiences here. It is something of a haven for walkers and hikers, and one can imagine a dog passing through the back fields with its routed paths, wandering in search of a safe space to call home – looking for the ancient in the midst of the transient, seeking a sanctuary in which to draw breath and stay alive.

The farm was hemmed in by some heavily matured trees, yet the horizon could still be seen beyond them, against a blue sky infiltrated by the white-line remnants of recently departed clouds. In decades past, the surrounding hillsides had all been farmland. The majority of the farmers had made a reasonable living without needing to supplement their income with additional jobs and working sheepdogs had been kept busy, managing herds on a daily basis. But that was before. The landscape may not have changed much over time, and there was a sense of eternity to the region largely due to a lack of industry, but the farm itself was in need of immediate repair.

'Anne, what's the story with the collapsed roof?' I asked, before the moment ceded – as if the sky had fallen in and the ground was littered with clouds – to a black and white blob. My eyes adjusted to a picture slowly making its form apparent: a sheepdog. The dog's tail was moving back and forward at such a rate it was nearly banging against his head. It was a full-body shuffle more than a straightforward tail wag. I hunched down, brushing my hand against the matted clots in his coat, to rub the dog's stomach. In the photograph, his tentative stare had gripped my attention, but now he was looking at me in a completely unexpected fashion: this dog who was so infused with the joy of life. Since Anne mentioned 'stray' and 'rescue' in the office, my mind had been consumed with thoughts of a disgruntled dog, in fear of human contact and in need of care. This was set alongside an image that had braced my attention as a child: that of an angry, growling dog, afraid of every move – an animal terrorised by fear. Suddenly, against those ferocious impressions, here was the friendliest dog I had ever set eyes on.

Oscar was jumping on his back legs before lying down again, placing the side of his face against the ground – a pose I later read is a typical collie mannerism – his tail wagging and eyes staring with intent. He rubbed his face along the ground before jumping up again. My initial concern – that the dog who was living in the shed would need to be coaxed out with canine treats – was shattered by his electric movement, the fact that he was so enamoured with contact, so taken with humans. His introduction was overwhelming. We fed him treats on the cobblestones – sausages, which he ate slowly – while we examined the shed he had made his home. A little battered bowl, half-filled with multicoloured kibble, stood out against a concrete floor littered with discarded farm materials. Weeds had begun shooting up from cracks in the concrete, as if nature was reclaiming the space for itself. The farm seemed to have lost its way, to have stopped battling the ageing imprint of years that had passed.

The growth was most conspicuous on the main house of the shrouded estate. The house was a trace of the British ascendancy's determining presence in Ireland. It was built in

The abandoned farm near Kilkishen where Oscar was living.

1846 – a century or more before it fell into the hands of the descendent bachelor farmer whom I was told was now in the throes of dementia – it was originally registered as the estate of Henry Thomas Baylee. The estate was too big a repair job for the present owner, an irony given that a Baylee daughter, and former proprietor of the estate, married Percy le Clerc, one of the leading architects of his time and known countrywide for restoring property; Holycross Abbey and Bunratty Castle form part of his extended portfolio. Bunratty, as it is referred to in Ireland, is one of most visited sites in East Clare, the castle itself a pool of historical curiosity. A theme park, restaurants and shops have sprung up in recent decades to support the tourist trade, with the castle having become a landmark so familiar that I hardly notice it when I set out along the road for Cloondarone.

Stationed just off the motorway in the village of Bunratty is the castle site, dating back to the beginnings of Christian Ireland and intricately associated with ancient and colonial rule. The castle was a site of interest to the Kingdom of Thomond, a geographical region that included Limerick and Clare. In the fourteenth century, it took form in its current shape and, three centuries later, the building was of notable concern during the Confederate War, a major conflict between Catholics and Dublin Castle, the colonial stronghold in the country. During the war, which lasted nearly ten years, Bunratty was taken over by Barnabas O'Brien, the sixth Earl of Thomond, who tried to stay neutral in the proceedings. He was later in contact with the notorious Henry Cromwell, who led a reign of terror throughout the region. By the nineteenth

century, the residence had entered into a state of disrepair, with the roof falling in. For some time, it sank into ruination, before its restoration by Percy le Clerc. The site is a penny dropped into an ocean of time, encasing Ireland's history in the structure of its ancient stone.

The sheepdog at my feet had made it to this corner of rural Ireland – a place touched by the once-dominant classes on the island, now in retreat. It was a world that still existed on the margins of everyday life, a walled-in oasis in a sea of ancient and mythical beauty, a site where British colonialism reached early Christian and pagan Ireland, mixing with everything else in between. Peering across the landscape, the lake sparkling against a turning light, cottages sat quietly on the hills, lit up with green and yellow hues from the setting sun – seductive cues for the wandering eye. A ruined castle of sorts lay dormant on the horizon, across which was a row of Bungalow Bliss houses, small one-storey constructions that mushroomed as part of Ireland's modernisation in the '70s. The light fell on the houses, forming a bristle of shadows and silhouettes. A hazy wind blew across the field, gusting along the lake past bleating sheep in a pastoral haven, calling out like sirens to the slowly intruding night.

How did Oscar get here? What had brought him to an abandoned farm? Anne had already relayed the story about the farmer's debilitating dementia and how the estate had advanced into disrepair. Yet, for all its shortcomings, this was Oscar's shed, his secure and safe space. Perhaps it simply was his place. Maybe he was the old farmer's dog. It had been a working farm, after all, in one of the biggest sheep-farming regions: a site embedded with agricultural tradition. It turns out I would never fully ascertain how Oscar came to live there: whether he belonged to the farmer who had sadly entered a nursing home or whether he had made his way to the farm after it fell into decline.

As I looked all around the space, Anton was fidgeting. Both of us were struggling to get our bearings, consumed by Oscar's powers of exertion. Anne was waiting for an answer. She wanted to know if I would take him, not necessarily that evening, but in a few days. Hesitant at first, I quickly made up my mind. I confirmed we would adopt him and collect him at the weekend. There was nothing more to do, other than to bring him home as part of the family. Work commitments meant stalling for a few days, until the Sunday of the coming weekend, to collect him. That is, assuming he didn't run away in the meantime. But just as we were about to return to the car, he began to follow in the same direction. I felt the urge to bring him with us that very moment. It was an all-encompassing desire.

Instead, I said 'stay' repeatedly. He turned and hunkered at the gate, eyeballing me with a stare that induced a degree of guilt on my behalf. My urge to care for him, to shelter him from the threat of the wild beyond those walls, was overbearing. It was hard to push back the image of his face between the steel gate, whimpering like a child who misses his mother. In the years that followed that first visit, I would often look back and berate myself for leaving him exposed to the savagery of a world outside the safety of the farm – and one impervious to his goodness. But I had not planned to take him with us that day and the necessary elements to bring him home were not in place; there were no supplies to nurture him. I thought it best not to disturb Oscar any more than was necessary at that given moment. But when we got back to the car, thinking that the land had called out to us, it suddenly felt like the visit returned a resounding 'Yes!'

The light had yet to fully dim on the drive over county lines as night called, a warm wind gusting in the window, confirming summer's arrival. Ylva was at the stairs when we got home, coaxing Karl to sleep. It was almost dark as we sprinted inside, pushing into a quiet room to report on the evening.

'It's strange,' I said. 'It feels like he was dropped on my lap from above. I've never met an animal that is so infused with life. It's hard to believe he's a stray, abandoned or whatever happened to him.'

Then Anton chimed in. 'You should have heard him whimpering as we were leaving. He lay on his stomach and cried like he had known us for ever.'

My wife smiled while nodding in confirmation. An air of excitement began to fill the room. The rest of the week would be taken up sourcing provisions and equipment, preparing for Oscar the sheepdog to arrive home.

The local pet shop yielded the basics: kibble and a bowl to eat and drink from; a sleeping basket; a new, more collie-friendly collar; and a lead to help domesticate him. Our house sits beside Glenstal Abbey, a former landed estate now home to a Benedictine Order on the edge of Murroe. We are located just around the corner from the front gates to the monastery and hoped to soon walk Oscar through the monastery grounds. He would need, however, to look like a respectable pet to do so, capable of walking on a lead. In anticipation, I stocked up on doggie treats to begin the lessons, thinking ahead to a time when, walking the trails, he would instantly return to me through call alone. Until then, however, the do's and don'ts had to be ticked off one by one, the things to keep a pet in check. I rang Anne on Saturday to let her know we would be coming the next day. She offered to collect Oscar from the farm, meaning we could pick him up from her place on the Sunday evening. It made it all so much easier.

On Sunday, two cars were needed to transport several family members. Ylva took Anton and my mum, who was visiting for the weekend, while Karl and I travelled in another car. On the second journey to Kilkishen, with the ruins of Kilkishen Castle standing up like a gift from the gods in the distance, *Blood on the Tracks* came on the stereo again. I told Karl that I often sang the opening lines from 'Idiot Wind' – one of the most iconic songs on what many believe to be Dylan's best album – to his mum when we started dating, explaining the importance of the song to the origin of our family. And now here we were on our way to an old countryside farm together to rescue a sheepdog. Life was straightforward again. All our attention was concentrated on a simple act, a collective family occasion. The silhouette of the castle could still be glimpsed from the side road as the car slowed to turn as 'Shelter from the Storm' played from the car speakers.

It is one of the most-cherished Dylan songs. It consists of a three-chord progression played on an acoustic guitar, over which the verse rings out. *Blood on the Tracks* is an album about the tumultuous breakdown of Dylan's marriage to his wife, Sara, and 'Shelter from the Storm' reads like one long lyrical struggle. An everyman figure, looking for shelter from a raging storm, takes refuge with a woman. In one sense an allegory surrounding Dylan's personal struggles at the time, it is also something else: a furtive insight into the depths of the human condition. The image of a woman offering care to a weather-beaten man, during an actual storm that doubles as an emotional one, taps into the human instinct to care. 'In a world of steel-eyed death, and men who are fighting to be warm,' Dylan sings, inviting the refrain, '"Come in," she said, "I'll give you shelter from the storm."' The car pushed headlong into the wind, with the magnetic sun drawing the family towards clouds sat upon mountains and the song reaching into the depths of my gut. I imagined this exuberant, larger-than-life animal, beaten and abandoned in cruel circumstances, banished from the nearby village. And then I thought of the photograph Anne had sent of Oscar peering out through a shed doorway. Was I the woman in Dylan's 'Shelter . . .' – a carer of forsaken souls in the midst of a ravaged earth?

As the song gathered momentum, a lone tear crept down my cheek. Maybe it was the idea of collecting a living being, a dog so enraptured by the mere presence of humans, that captivated me. Or maybe the tear was a mark of something greater even again: all the memories of driving with my father to Galway as a child – moments that seemed ordinary and fleeting at the time, yet were remembered as extraordinary. Just as Karl was enthralled by the landscape unfolding beyond the grey tarmac of the road, I too had once sat enchanted in the passenger seat as my father drove, selecting cassettes to play to light up the mood and staring out at the west with its infamous stone walls. The N17, a road no longer the main route from Tuam to Galway, is used today by those who resist the lure of the motorway. Like so many roads, its design masks the plethora of minor roads that act as tributaries to it, small vistas that lead into the mystery and singularity of the parish, each one with its individual lure. In one such parish, a sheepdog named Oscar had made himself home and, in travelling to collect him from this home, the rescue act was in process. But the drive was also an act of discovery, one that replicated so many from my youth.

'Take care' was such a common Irish saying, especially on wishing someone well. 'Take care driving,' my mother will often say to me, like a blessing. But, as I surveyed the rolling hills beside the motorway, I thought again of the care taken in offering shelter, in bringing home a sheepdog that had appeared magically, like an angel masking its true purpose and design. To 'take care' was to pluck magic beans from the sky, like something stolen from another world, a world better and safer than ours.

Dylan's song played over again, with each line nudging me closer to the idea that to care for a dog could somehow become a panacea for the physical shock that had consumed me that year. In three weeks' time, I would be standing at the back of a church marking the anniversary of my father's death. Grief had come in unexpected moments, incisions interrupting the struggle to understand. That struggle would lessen in time, of course. But on the drive to the country to collect a sheepdog from a farm, one major want was pushing through in me: to return life to the world. Our intentions were centred on a sharpening will in the pull of desire – the solace to be found deep in the soul of the countryside. To shelter this gregarious bundle of joy would soon become my calling.

The sound of Dylan's voice spilled out into the breeze, pushing through a window like a stream of unfiltered affection. My storm was sudden death: clouds that descend in an instant; a farm, horses, a dog, a cat; an estate only the deceased knew how to run; a son who knew little about the intricacies of farming life; a scatter of hangers-on claiming to be his close friends. How to know? How to distinguish? Where to find shelter? And, beyond the practicalities of death, were other questions that would not relent. *Where are you? Where did you go?* Caught in a storm of unanswered questions, I glanced over at the child in the passenger seat, a boy learning to comprehend the world around a shared purpose – to source some meaning in a storm of complicated emotions, one that had descended upon those driving in two cars.

The convoy moved in sync, pushing into wind, past gorse, overladen hedges, elements of nature soon to be in bloom. The hills of Clare, meshed in summer colour, returned my thinking to Bruegel's masterpiece *The Hunters in the Snow*. For years, I had been preoccupied with the meaning of the winter scene – the pictorial cautioning against a powerful ability to affect. In the painting, peaks and valleys roll under a carpet of winter, hills that hold the hunters giving way to a valley, beyond which gangs of children are seen skating on ice. The perspective is a key to understanding the scene: the hunters are mere silhouettes monitored from behind; the spectacular snow-covered hills are devoid of animal life. Dogs accompany the hunters, one of whom carries a dead fox on his back, and all of them stare at the snow, hunching down in forward motion, demoralised by the cold. The trees are barren; a single crow, a symbol of death, hovers overhead; a woman flays a pig, a tradition associated with peasant life in the Netherlands. Below, in the distant valley, peasants wait on hunters tasked with scavenging for food in times of scarcity amidst the ravages of winter. In the picture's composition, the scene foregrounds the hunters, while the peasants whose leisure relies on their pursuits are far away in the distance, the landscape of the once-fertile valley that they will work in warmer months engulfing them.

As a professor of cinema, the painting holds a special meaning for me. I began my doctoral studies exploring the moral treatment of evil by filmmakers, consumed by the films of Pier Paolo Pasolini and Robert Bresson. Over time, I was drawn more to landscape and the way emotions are invested in the earth as part of broader ethnographic pursuits. I began exploring these issues in films like *sleep furiously* (2008), a faux documentary directed by Gideon Koppel about a small village in mid-Wales and Abbas Kiarostami's *The Wind Will Carry Us* from 1999, a film that investigates a moment of epiphany in the northern Iranian landscape.

Pieter Bruegel the Elder, *The Hunters in the Snow* (1565)
Kunsthistorisches Museum, Vienna
© Kate Kimber / Alamy

I found Koppel's film, although not explicitly about the filmmaker's mother, to be movingly so. The land was a key character in both films, the imagery fleshing out the connection between the emotions and the seasons. Russian filmmaker Andrei Tarkovsky hung a print of *The Hunters in the Snow* on the Soviet spaceship in his sci-fi masterpiece *Solaris* to emphasise this very point. In his later autofictional film *Mirror* – my all-time favourite – the painting's depiction of hills and valleys comes to life as a scene from Tarkovsky's childhood during the war.

As we drove to Kilkishen that second evening, the painting's auratic meaning seemed to reach out to me anew. Imagining the disgruntled hunters returning from the hunt seemed to mirror my own journey that calendar year. I too had become a hunter searching, looking for existential truth: where does the soul go when the body dies? It seemed a heavy storm of melancholic maladjustment: the weight of grief is to look and not find.

I fiddled around with the stereo so that 'Shelter from the Storm' played on repeat. Thoughts of Dylan and Bruegel synced as if designed to fall together. Karl nonchalantly gazed out the window, fixated on traces of Ylva and the others moving in the distance. I stopped the car at a ditch on a byroad to stretch my legs. A murmuration of starlings fluttered across a field; a ruined cottage sat in one corner, a group of cattle in the other. A light brown cow munching on grass peered in my direction. I winked back. A near-motionless landscape greeted me like a screen of discarded objects, my eyes tripping over wild stumps of grass that grew out from stone wall crevices. I swung around to the front of the car to get the journey going again. Once the car ignition triggered and the lights came on, the music began to play again. This time, however, instead of ushering me into the world of *The Hunters in the Snow*, I awoke to a different season. No longer ensconced in winter's snow. Instead, a glaring sun reached out towards me.

We were at a junction before taking the road to where Oscar was waiting. A field to our left was littered with haystacks, a rare display in the Irish landscape given the changes to agriculture in decades past. Haystacks have been replaced – en masse – with synthetic parcels of silage produced by machines. In view of the former, another – later – Bruegel painting, *The Harvesters*, came to mind. It is a homage to summer. Unlike the silhouetted hunters with their faces hidden, the harvesters are depicted on wood panels on a much bigger scale, more easily discerned by the viewer. Like *The Hunters in the Snow*, *The Harvesters* is a painting that encourages the gaze of the beholder to wander from a height, a point where peasants are resting from the summer sun to a place where hay is harvested. The gaze moves along the horizon line to the valleys, where children play in parks. Beyond the harvest is the sea, the ships like dots on a mystical expanse of ocean. Unlike the real Netherlands, which is famously flat, Bruegel's landscape is an imaginary place of deep peaks and valleys.

Our car slowed to a snail's pace as I peered over at the haystacks standing like sculptures made specifically for this parcel of land. I imagined the fields populated by families, communities coming together to make the winter

Pieter Bruegel the Elder, *The Harvesters* (1565)
The Metropolitan Museum of Art, New York,
Rogers Fund, 1919

manageable for animals and humans alike. My mind pressed upon a network of memories: Indian summers spent deep in the throes of labour and long afternoons turning turf. Then I thought of the vital activities purporting to be of the Irish landscape that had died with the onset of the industrial and then information age.

The Harvesters is a homage to labour, to the land. Years of suburban dwelling had severed my link to the countryside. I came to the painting in its pictorial simplicity as an invocation of days growing up in rural Ireland: evenings spent throwing bales of hay to passing trucks; the jokes, the thirst, the feeling of working on something greater than the individual – the earth. My memory of evenings spent waiting for the go-ahead to hit the town ignited – the end of harvest with its sensations intact: a smell in the air, a gush of pollinated flowers, a hazy breeze when sunburn fizzled on reddened cheeks. We were en route to rescue a sheepdog named Oscar. It felt right. The year was fresh with purpose – to safeguard a sheepdog from the perils of the world.

Anne's cottage overlooked a Bruegel-like lake. Just as our convoy arrived, she came out smiling to greet us. My mother opened the car door and happily made her way over to Anne. Then two more doors opened in a moment of synchronicity as Ylva and the two boys stepped away from the cars in antic-ipation of the change that lay ahead. I removed the collar and lead from the glove compartment and turned my gaze over my shoulder to see Karl standing tentatively away from the car. Our reckoning had come – Oscar would return with us. Mum and Anne were deep in conversation beside the front gate and Ylva was waving across to Karl and me. Along the path, hedges ringed the surrounding heather in harmony, with the yellow-infused gorse standing out like dabs of paint on stretched canvas. The odour of cattle manure filtered through the air while the sound of machinery in the distant fields echoed beyond. The area was a hive of unfettered nature. I strolled over to where Anne and Ylva were now standing, over from my mother and the two boys, to excitedly wait with them for the big moment to arrive.

'I'll go to get him,' Anne said and we nodded back in agreement. 'Just try not to overwhelm him.' Then she took off to the side of her cottage. Thirty seconds later, she returned with a ragged sheepdog.

Oscar was pulling hard on the lead, dragging Anne along with him. He was so low to the ground it was difficult to recognise the contours of a particular species. Then he began to assess the space around him, in a frenzy of excitement, unnerving my mother so much she retreated to the car. We formed a small circle around him. His tail was moving so frantically that it was banging against his head just like I had seen before. Away from the farmyard, Oscar's demeanour was that of an abandoned animal cast adrift in a world, made to fend for himself, his tangled mat part of an unexpectedly dishevelled appearance. I stood back, looking over his body with some discomfort, my earlier unease returning with renewed vigour.

'We'll have to get him into the car, Anne,' I said, before Ylva instantly replied, 'I'll hold him.'

My failure to show a similar readiness to carry him haunted

me for a long time after – I didn't trust my instinct to hold Oscar in my arms. Why was I afraid? Why was I holding back, allowing others to do the job? The truth is I was haunted by an advert from national TV as a child. In the advert, a rabies-infested dog is cornered. When a hand is shown reaching to comfort the dog, the creature bares its teeth aggressively, before building into a full-blooded attack. The advert was meant to encourage dog owners to get their dogs vaccinated. But, for me, it was an early exposure to animal violence that stayed with me long after. Instead of holding Oscar in the car to let him know he was safe and allowing Ylva to drive, I took refuge in the driver's seat. My mother had to drive Anton and Karl home.

'Some dogs don't like to be lifted,' Anne muttered while I stared at one that was cowering in fear, before swinging the door open and dangling a piece of 'deer meat' seductively in front of him.

'Think he's ever been in a car?' I said to Anne when confronted for the first time with the size of the task. Maybe Oscar was a feral of sorts.

'Probably not,' Anne said forcefully, before Ylva rose to the task of handling Oscar, allowing me to mask my fear. It was a decision on my wife's part that I think Oscar remembers, such is the affection he has for her to this day. In many ways, I think he sees her as his protector.

Ten minutes were taken up bundling a medium-sized, terrified sheepdog into the back of a Toyota. Oscar jumped away at first, sliding his body underneath the rear of the car. He shivered as I offered him a small twig and attempted to coax him out towards the deer treats. I was trying, throughout, to be as gentle as possible with him.

'Is he afraid?' I asked Anne, appearing confident when I was likely to be the one most afraid.

'No, no,' Anne replied. 'He's probably just had a really tough few weeks.'

Eventually he was lured out from under the car using dog treats. We backed up hastily to give him enough space to jump into the passenger seat in pursuit of the treat placed on it.

'If you let down the front seat and climb into the back that way, Ylva, we'll get him in,' I said, appearing to be in control of things when it was anything but the case. Then I motioned to Anne to close the door. Suddenly, he was in.

We had to get on the road as swiftly as possible. Gesturing over at the others to jump in quickly, I called out 'Thanks for everything – I'll be in touch soon' in Anne's direction as Ylva squeezed into the back seat while petting Oscar. A puddle of drool formed on the floor. As soon as the car began to move, the dribble increased and Ylva – having had little or no preparation – was unable to stop it. She spoke to Oscar in Swedish, using phrases I hadn't heard since our children were toddlers. (Ylva's shift into Swedish, that first real communication with Oscar, would have a lasting impact. For years, I began to practise – without dwelling on the decision – pidgin Swedish with Oscar. It was only when watching videos of us together that I finally realised what I was doing.) The car pushed against the rays of evening sun, the landscape stretching out in front, as I constantly enquired about how Oscar was doing in the back seat.

The return home was a blur – one of those drives when details glaze over into a daze, when experience flows so fast all context evaporates. Oscar's head lurched backwards and forwards, as he stared at the floor. Ylva stroked his coat, whispering that everything would be okay, he was safe. Not to overcomplicate was one of her many admirable qualities. The lyrics of 'Shelter from the Storm' pushed into my thoughts, the silhouettes from *The Hunters in the Snow* an accompanying visual. I imagined the woman flaying a pig offering sustenance to hunters. Was Oscar getting similar sustenance from a woman he had only just met? On the slow drive home, the mountains appeared aloof in the diminishing light and an odour of recently spread silage from adjacent farms filtered in through the window. And then, just as the car made its way up the driveway to our house, worries returned with vengeance: *What were we taking on? Why had we signed up for this? What state was Oscar really in?* But my mother and the boys were waiting. Anton was holding a lead, ready to show Oscar the expanses of the field adjacent to our house. I stepped out of the car as the door swung open. Oscar jumped out as the group appeared, primed to reveal to him all the home wonders.

But the dog that ventured into the yard that evening bore little resemblance to the joyful mess that had first appeared on the hillside farmyard a few days earlier. He was subdued, out of kilter. Before I had time to consider why, he had already made his way underneath the engine. My imagined strolls in the runaway pastures of home, with a domesticated sheepdog at my beck and command, were destroyed in an instant. I used a stick to gently prod at Oscar to get him out.

'He's probably scared,' I declared, attempting to puncture the disappointment and coax him slowly. 'It's obvious he's never been in a car before,' I said to my mother who was trying – at the same time – not to irritate in offering advice but managing to irritate me by quizzically asking, 'Are you sure you know what you're doing?' Of course, I had no idea what I was doing. That was why I was leaning underneath the car, jabbing at Oscar to come out. Before I had prodded him with any major intent, Oscar crawled out and scuttled over towards the lawn, stretching out in a submissive pose.

'Get the lead on him,' I shouted over to the group, seeing Ylva was hunched in a squat-like position. 'Quick, before he runs away and into the field.'

A human chain circled around a frightened dog who shuffled onto the lawn, his head bowed down.

'Why isn't he excited like he was before?' Anton asked inquisitively, to which there was no immediate and obvious answer. I googled 'rescue dog comes home for first time. What next?' on my phone. By the time answers appeared, Ylva had begun to walk Oscar around the garden's tree-heavy boundary as the group stared in awe. He had no concept of being on a lead and his neck, hemmed in so that he was pulling awkwardly in all directions, jerked him forward. So much of what had seemed normal on the farm – his size, his appearance – now stood out, like his matted coat. He looked like anything but a domesticated pet. It was as though he had fallen from some wild, godforsaken land. The initial thrill on finding him dissipated.

Oscar bowed his head, the crusts of mud dangling from his

long-haired coat. Clouds began to gather above and the rain threatened a sudden downpour. The collective began to run for cover. I ran over to help Ylva escort Oscar into the patio room, the 'one-bedroom apartment' we had put in place for him that weekend, leading up to his first big day at home.

Our house, in its present form, had taken shape in increments, over several decades. The original 1960s build was extended in the '70s, making two points of entry. One looks out at leylandii trees that bookend a path leading out to the field of a local farmer, Frank Ryan. Bay windows open to a view of the Silvermine Mountains from the rear entrance, sheltering the patio room. A little heater sits in the corner of the patio for cold nights, beside which we placed a basket and cushions for a medium-sized dog. Considerable time had been spent making the patio as appealing for a new guest as possible.

As we sheltered from the storm, my repressed fears, pushed under my skin, began to surface as new responsibilities. He didn't seem like the dog we had met before. This wasn't the rescue I'd imagined.

But it was, of course, the same dog. It was just the context that had changed. At the farm, animals were in direct earshot and the place had a rundown 'farm' feel. It was normal for an unkempt sheepdog to be seen roaming around. Go to any Irish farm and similarly uncouth working dogs will stare up at you. That first evening on the farm, the hills had been luscious in beauty. We breathed the summer air into our furtive lungs, as if it were the scene of a Dylan Thomas poem. Life reached a pitch of mystical perfection, captivating as an experience. A part of me had been seduced by the romanticism of it all, enthralled by the splendour of the countryside. The evening had lent itself to poetic musings: images of man and nature in symbiosis.

But the return home changed things. Reality intervened. I watched a scared, perhaps traumatised animal walk tentatively around the leylandii-enclosed garden, with my mother, wife and children looking on, wondering if I was in the right frame of mind to care for him. The warning that 'a dog is for life' was now a missile hitting its target. My life was rocked. I was struggling to care for myself and lacked the concentration and due diligence to take on the responsibility. It felt too much.

2

A Kind of Revival

Oscar's first and second evenings were subdued. Settled to a degree, he remained devoid of the life force we had encountered on the farm. My initial concern was that he would bark to get out of the patio room, waking up our 89-year-old neighbour Michael, from whom we had bought the house just six months earlier. Obviously nobody wanted this to happen. No one wanted Oscar to end up in a pound or a rescue centre. It was hard to countenance ever having to do something so drastic, but there was serious concern that he would wake Michael up at night. But he never barked for that first week. Nor did he bark the first month – or year. That first evening, against the flow of catastrophic projections, Oscar remained silent. He slept on the opposite side of the patio room to where the bed lay and didn't open his mouth to make a single sound. He was tired. When peering in, I saw him sprawled out on the bare floor. All the hours spent choosing the right bed, the eventual decision to go with a hand-woven basket, was of little worth; when the moment arrived, Oscar was impervious to the fact it was his.

The next day, I rang a friend who volunteers with Limerick Animal Welfare. I was looking for some basic advice about dog behaviour, as I was worried about Oscar's subdued demeanour. Several cues came from our initial chat. First, the whole experience had been tiring for Oscar. Fatigue had overwhelmed him that evening. Second, it was a kind of trauma, this act of removing him from the farm that had been his safe space. My friend pointed out that Oscar had probably never been in a car, was unlikely to have been microchipped and was probably riddled with fleas and worms. He told me to take him to a vet and a groomer, and to put wheels of nourishment in motion. The advice made sense. Instead of a high-energy response to deep stress, such as like the shake-up from fleeing quickly or a tentative expression of fear, it was at first hard to identify the trauma in Oscar because his initial response took the opposite form.

It would become apparent in time that his submissiveness was part of a general nervousness that was typical of collies. At the farm, Oscar's electric movement and sheer delight in making contact with a human other masked his nervousness, manifesting in a need to illustrate that he wasn't a threat to me. This 'need' is hard to explain, in that it exposed the kind of awareness he seemed to have of the threat his species withhold. Taken as a kind of communication, it is hard not to read this as a plea. But just because a dog displays submissive behaviour in one situation does not mean they will be submissive in every one. This, surely, was true of Oscar. Don't be fooled. He has a steeliness about him, having survived for many weeks on a farm alone.

Some months after his rescue, I watched Oscar race in through the trees to return to the patio room from the back field, populated with rabbits, where he could wander safely for a small distance. He was holding something in his mouth that I had to pluck out with my hand. As I felt the object, I soon realised I was holding the butt of a rabbit, its furry tail brushing against my fingers. I understood that Oscar was well able to fend for himself, and was independent even when lacking in human contact.

On the day of the visit to the groomer, however, he still had to be coaxed into a car with towels and treats, the former to take the hit of constant drooling. It would be my first visit to a dog groomer and I had no real idea what they did. The Ireland of my youth had little by way of dog grooming businesses. Indeed, the culture of keeping pets in twenty-first-century Ireland was new to me. Irish families in the '80s could just about afford to feed a dog, never mind professionally groom them. The pet world had changed beyond all recognition.

I arrived at the groomer's – a Geordie man who was married to an Irish woman living near to Newport in Tipperary – with very little understanding of the grooming profession. Once John appeared alone, however, I knew within minutes I was in the presence of a proper dog lover (of German shepherds in particular). He led Oscar into a garage that was given over to his grooming work and then set about easing my concerns, stressing that Oscar needed a good combing and washing down. John assured me that the dog was just in an adjustment phase after leaving the farm, a place where he had felt safe and secure. After chatting a little, and once the grooming work had begun in earnest, I was told to return in about three hours to collect Oscar.

A short distance from John's house, on the Limerick–Murroe road, was an accessible riverside walk. A line of cherry blossom near the road fell into a wet depression that marked a sudden transformation in the landscape and a field of grazing sheep faced a wet marshy bog. I parked, removed a small cushion from the car boot and set off with a bag, sunglasses and a book, with the plan of sitting in the sun for an hour or two by the River Mulcair. I had assumed the grooming time would take an hour or possibly two, but never three. In the distance, a farmer was ushering cattle towards a gate, accompanied by a teenage boy I assumed to be his son. The cattle appeared to me as dabs of colour in the glowing sunshine, the field a moving frame of composition. It was a pastoral scene encountered every day in rural Ireland. As it appeared, the scene triggered a memory of the evening prior to news breaking about my father's accident. We were making our way home from Ballybunion Beach. A farmer appeared in front of me moving cattle from one field to the next, signalling to drivers to slow down. As I brought the car to a standstill, I turned to the kids and joked that we were 'caught in traffic'. The cattle rolled by the window as I took a moment to glance at my phone. There was a missed call, emblazoned with the word 'Dad'. For a moment, I thought of returning it. But it was a long way home from the beach. We were tired and it could wait.

Weeks of dwelling on not returning his call passed, wondering whether it might have changed the scheme of events and thus the course of time. The conversation might have broken the causal chain. The fatal accident leading to my father's passing might have been avoided; my answer might have made a difference. But the response was never triggered and time took its fatalistic course. Maybe, I reasoned, he would call back. But an hour after returning home, I was manning a barbecue; sun-scorched kids running circles around me. I never rang him, never made that call. A year or so had passed since that day and I now sat by the Mulcair, the water lulling my senses, all my attention consumed with questions that would never be answered. Where are *you*? Where have *you* taken leave for?

There was some time remaining before John finished grooming. The plan was to walk the riverbank for a few hundred yards, as far as to where the current gathered in strength. On the other side of a wall where the riverside path seemed to end, a field was littered with sheep and newborn lambs. There must have been fifty or so in a field that was three or four, or possibly five, acres wide. It was a pastoral haven, a fertile expression of nature set with human hands. Ewes were feeding newborn offspring, while more lambs lolled in the grass.

The scene prompted me to remember a lecture I had attended somewhere, either as a graduate student at the University of Exeter or after. A newly appointed professor was giving an inaugural lecture, a tradition for appointments to the chair. She was talking about care, a research area pioneered by the feminist Carol Gilligan. Attendees were packed in a stuffy theatre, overheated by human bodies. Beads of sweat trickled down the front of my brow as the professor began to address the crowd about the ethics of 'care'. Care cultivates life as interdependent. Care, the audience were told that day, cultivates the ethical plurality of being. It was an ethics that feminists turned to in the '80s.

Feminism, as I understood it back then, was the struggle for equality among the sexes, not a way of caring for another person relationally and ethically. Care as a condition of interdependent beings stayed with me long after as a conceptual concern; care as a source of love. Ancillary claims that same day were made in tandem with a theory premised on differences of 'emotional' and 'rational' knowledge: males are taken in by abstraction, rights and justice, contrasting feminine emphasis on nurturing relationships. Males are drawn to logic and reason, the feminine to emotional relations. Gilligan's ethics have since been regarded as essentialist by some, her research deemed to be reductive around the distinction 'man' and 'woman', but none of this seemed to impact upon me when peering into a field. Ewes were caring for lambs, as I waited on a sheepdog.

Over the course of that year following Dad's death, difficult thoughts, often hazy and unclear, would break through at inopportune moments, as if the membrane designed to stop emotions overwhelming us had given way. Music triggered something, like a retention of time spent with my father. U2's album *The Joshua Tree* was a case in point, summoning memories so vivid it was like I could reach out to touch him from up close. He was there but, of course, he was not. Grief was the word used to describe this experience, when involuntary remembering cultivates desire, never met, to reach out and hold. I lost count of the times I played 'Running to Stand Still' from that album that first year, each time the song striking like a hammer to the gut. Yet each time, I sought out the hammer – sought out feelings to counter the numbness that had encased my body from the moment the news of my father's death broke.

The Joshua Tree is an album largely driven by international concerns, yet I was drawn to that particular song, the fifth on the album, because of its deep resonance with the mood of '80s Ireland. Very much a depiction of Dublin's Ballymun district, it is a powerful protest. The two heroin addicts whose story is told in the song, their lives centred on the momentary transcendence of an opiate high, spoke to me of grieving: those brief interludes of feeling that were craved by my grieving self in order to pass through them. Sometimes, the tears flooded in, like a tsunami of unheralded emotion, only to dry up as though under a desert sun. '"Running to Stand Still" is for anyone who feels trapped in an impossible circumstance by overwhelming responsibility,' Mark Flanagan wrote in the liner notes for the twentieth anniversary album edition, a reading that aligns closely with my later understanding. The loss of my father, especially as an only son, often felt like an 'overwhelming responsibility', one that got in the way of feelings. It obstructed feeling the necessary emotion to eventually meet acceptance. It delayed the finality, catching me in the turbulent adrenaline required to get things done, pushed to adapt to the changing practicalities of life when someone has died.

The hazy memory of the inaugural address at Exeter, was a cue to think about nourishing care. Taking care would reduce the seeking that feeds grieving. Perhaps, in the throes of the care relationship, a differing source of knowledge would reveal itself to me. To care would beg the question: where is the line between emotion and reason? Or truth?

As I turned away from the field of lambs that day to peer into the river and its translucent water, shades of blue touched upon effervescent green. The river sparkled with the blush of an awakening sunshine. Baby trout spun back and forth as nature began to cradle me in its grasp. Then a trickle of rain pushed down through clouds. The time had come to collect Oscar. Nestled under a wall – with just enough shelter to see the phone screen – I texted John to make sure it was okay. Minutes later, he replied that Oscar would be ready to leave in half an hour.

Walking back along the rain-sodden riverbank that afternoon, cherry blossom dropping newly formed petals, I began to imagine a no-longer-ragged sheepdog. A couple and child advanced in my direction, hands signalling hello. In a rush to yield to the vibrant thoughts of care, I returned a smile and walked on with a blissful intent. I was the woman in 'Shelter from the Storm'; I was Bruegel's muse calling to the hunters. All I could think about was Oscar.

At John's place, the words 'come on in' were heard echoing from the garage and grooming area. Once I got to the garage, the door opened to show Oscar at a table hemmed in by a metal harness. Clots of hair gathered across the wooden floor. A large beach-coloured German shepherd slept in a silver crate in the corner of the same room. He woke up to look in my direction, content for his master to do the dog-grooming honours with Oscar instead of him. Oscar's long coat had been transformed. He looked like he had months of good living to his name and was bristling with energy as a result.

'Such a great job you've done. Thanks a lot, John,' I said, handing him a trivial fee for three hours of intensive grooming work on Oscar. 'No bother at all,' John replied, before talking of his life as a painter and decorator, and of his enduring love of dogs. He had kept German shepherds for as long as he could recall, he said, first encountering the breed as a child. His family were breeders and had entered their dogs in competitions. As a result, he was educated from a very early age in the art of dog grooming for show.

John spoke of his lifelong battle with the medical condition osteogenesis, also known as 'brittle bones'. He had worked as a painter/decorator when able to manage his health condition accordingly, but age took its toll and his condition had worsened, ending his career. Dog grooming was not just a business, but a way of staying busy performing an activity he loved. It was his trust in the dogs laid out on his table that had impressed me the most, a trust he had invested readily in a sheepdog who was found living alone on a farm. I questioned him about Oscar, attempting to tap into the wisdom that came from having worked with dogs all his life.

'Is he okay?' I inquired. 'Do you think he has been abused?'

He shuffled about in his chair, accompanied by a silence. I waited for the conversation to gather pace but was instead met by a finger-to-thumb gesture as he suggested a cup of tea. Gesturing a thumbs-up in return, I took Oscar round to the front of the house to put him in the car. John arrived at the front minutes later with tea and biscuits. He spoke at length about working dogs, about the special temperament of German shepherds in particular. Although they are mostly co-opted as pets, he said, the breed has a longstanding working tradition as search-and-rescue dogs and even for herding. Like collies, he mentioned, winking at Oscar in the car, they are extremely intelligent. It was the first but not the last time that I would hear 'intelligence' used to describe the mentality of a dog. It was no doubt interesting, but as a discussion point it didn't seem that useful; we tend to think of human intelligence, which cannot be the same.

Two points John made to me that day lingered long after: these concerned submissiveness and companionship. In response to my query about abuse, he had subsequently explained that Oscar was very submissive. Some servile dogs have been treated badly, though not necessarily abused. It was not always the case that mistreatment bred aggression; such dogs are often too eager to please, manifesting in submissive behaviour. The way Oscar bends his head when he sees me – the way he gazes up with the side of his face touching the ground – is evocative of a submissive state. But it is evocative, John added, because collies are so attentive to command. They look to a handler for signals. He spoke about companionship as a defining but often underrated trait of working dogs. It was not that long ago that shepherds would spend weeks in the mountains, accompanied only by their dog. Oscar, he said, was that sort of dog. You can tell by his desire to please; by his movement and sensitivity to noise; by his 'eye' and 'bone'. 'Eye', I later learned, is the dog's capacity to control the prey animal with the stare, which has developed into a key attribute in herding as it near hypnotises the animal through the sheer strength of the gaze. Too much eye is prohibitive, I realised, scaring the sheep, but a touch is vital. 'Bone', on the other hand, is the dog's capacity to hold the sheep in a straight line, after circling the herd to get them into line. You can see the way Oscar hunches, John said to me, when staring forcefully. He was bred to make things happen with his eyes.

'Look over there,' John then concluded, pointing over at the Silvermine Mountains in the distance, Keeper Hill pushing up to the sky. 'He'll be your best friend up there.' As I gazed up at the mountain that lent a shadow over John that day, the talk of hills and trails began to excite me again. I had lost touch with hillwalking over the years; I couldn't even recall my last real mountain trek.

The Silvermines are a well-marked mountain range situated in north Tipperary, where the village of Silvermines is located, one rarely mentioned in the lexicon of Irish country life but which is perhaps close in its genesis and form to a typical Welsh mining village. Made up of numerous pathways and trails, the region is famous for its mining history and for its Devonian old red sandstone that appears like strange, near-exotic dust, often dominating the landscape. At the height of the so-called 'Celtic Tiger' period of the late '90s and 2000s – when Ireland was awash with new money and the surge of boom economics brought its own hysteria, reducing the state's longstanding poverty – Ylva and I travelled out to walk the trails that start at the back of the Silvermines village church. I remember looking around at the village, wondering what it had been like at the height of the twentieth century when the mining industry was surging in the region; its present decline was more akin to my hometown Tuam in the aftermath of the sugar factory closure. Distracted by these comparisons, I was nonetheless taken in by the distinct colour scheme of the landscape and the paths venturing up along the hills from behind the church.

For some reason, however, I had little interest in hiking at the time. I was too concentrated on some in-the-moment work thing, too caught up and absorbed in my life, too distracted by my career, so that my legs were heavy that day with Ylva. Or perhaps it was simply a lack of fitness. But my abiding memory of that Sunday-afternoon venture was a sense of disconnection from the landscape. Having lived in the suburbs for so long, I was numbed to the meditative entrancement of the countryside. I remember the sandy path, the sun beating down, the skyline that moved from Tipperary over into Limerick, the ache in my feet that prevented my ascent. Some said that the Silvermines had been mined since the thirteenth century and remain home to an assortment of minerals, including lead, zinc, copper and, according to some, silver; a fact that would pique my interest in discovering the region afresh someday. Perhaps it was time to revisit these mountains, now with Oscar by my side.

John repeated himself forcefully. 'He'll be a great companion. But it'll take time.'

And I really did believe him. Maybe the Geordie intonation

reassured me, or was it the passing of knowledge from one nation to another?

'How long?' I asked.

The sky was starting to change colour. A greyish black cloud was masking the sun. A virulent humidity was gathering in the air.

'Who knows?' he responded with something of a sigh. 'Bear in mind that Oscar once had a master. Time is needed to adjust to new surroundings. Everything's new. The more invested he was before, the longer it will take for a new attachment to form. His owner may not have been nice, who knows, but he was the only one Oscar knew.'

John's assertion that Oscar had had a master struck me profoundly. By 'master' I took him to mean he'd had a handler who might have been training him, or some work-related activity to that effect.

I turned John's words over on the drive home, as my new dog shivered in the back. The word 'companion' buzzed in my head like a fly on a summer night. Perhaps the time would come when the groomed sheepdog in the back seat would be content to run the trails with his new friend. I whispered to Oscar. But it was hard to know whether my words were of any real solace, whether repeating them over made any real difference.

We planned to walk a five-kilometre loop through the Glenstal estate with Oscar that evening, tapering back along the road to the village. The route moves through beautifully

manicured grounds; a man-made lake, home to a family of swans, sits on the right-hand side of the road, alongside acres of farmland to both the left and right inhabited by grazing cattle. Centuries-old trees stagger the long drive and, at the top, a little roundabout runs counter to a revivalist Norman castle, now the property of the Benedictine Order. A path leads from the former Barrington residence, part of the monastery, through the remainder of the grounds.

The Barringtons' legacy is significant to the Limerick district, such is their standing in the county as patrons. The revivalist Norman castle was built on the estate in the 1830s by Sir Matthew Barrington, who turned to a minor British architect, William Bardwell, for its style. In a move away from the popular Gothic-inspired houses of the time, Bardwell took inspiration from Penrhyn Castle in north Wales and Gosford Castle in County Armagh. The family, later under the tutelage of Sir Charles Barrington, resided at Glenstal until the mid-1920s, when the only daughter, Winifred, died unceremoniously in an IRA sabotage, an innocent victim in a brutal campaign to assert Irish sovereignty. The estate was then handed to the monks by a Catholic clergy member, Monsignor James Ryan, in 1925, after the War of Independence. The estate grounds have stayed true to their original design. Walkers pass sections of mature exotic forestry and a seating area where playing fields can be viewed from a prime position. After a kilometre, you exit the back gates onto a road that passes farmlands and country homes, residential areas and a school. It runs back to the village close to a football pitch and the pitch-and-putt course across from the gates of the abbey, five minutes from our home.

The route is busy throughout the year and is always open to the public. Walkers are asked to keep their dogs on a lead, the downside being that dogs become tense. Humans are asked to wear high-vis clothing, so the route is an outpouring of day-glo colour. As we set off, it was hard to take in the surroundings. The walkway was busy, with villagers out en masse to savour summer's arrival. Ylva held on to the lead as Oscar pulled in a perpetually forward movement. It was a struggle to contain his unbridled enthusiasm. But it was also clear to anyone with any understanding of dogs that he had never been walked in a domesticated fashion before – and it would take years for his eventual transformation into a pet. Lagging back to photograph the group from behind, I saw how Oscar awkwardly stood out. Friendly to those he met on the way, he was nonetheless unsure of himself. He dragged Ylva from one side of the road to the next, like a zigzagging rugby player making forward carries from the back of a ruck. The group was hunched. It was hard to say from our body language whether we were embarrassed or proud that a not-very-good-at-walking-on-a-lead sheepdog was part of our family.

Progress along the driveway was slow. The lake and swans stood out on our right, while lush pastures littered with cattle appeared on the left. At a certain point, Oscar flopped to the ground, refusing point-blank to budge. He crouched, his paws pushed out, his body horizontal, head resting on the road. I took the lead from Ylva to pull him on, but his body was immobile. I tried – in the sternest possible manner – to move him. I shouted, 'Oscar, move!' But he didn't react. Instead, he pushed his face sideways, staring ahead.

His stubbornness recalled a time in my youth when helping my father load a horse into a horsebox. A group huddled together in the yard beside the stables, another group nearby in support. It was a particularly stubborn horse that was clearly afraid of the horsebox. Just when it seemed there was no chance the horse would budge, even when gently whipped, he did a dance and trotted into the box without a bother. I thought about trying to do something similar with Oscar that would gently coax him along. But then I turned around to see a cow staring at us.

The cow was peering over the fence, quietly munching on grass. 'Don't tell me you're afraid, Oscar,' I said, trying to make light of the incident. 'Let's go back,' Ylva responded anxiously, as Anton muttered, 'Don't force him, Dad.' But instead of heeding their advice, I let the lead slip from my hand and pushed the cow to back off. Oscar retreated. There was little time to gesture at the cow to take a hike before Oscar tipped his tail against the electrified wire. He then ran away as fast as he could, running off in fear for his life. We were left standing on the road as evening walkers bustled past, while Oscar sprinted forth, first into an adjacent field and then on towards the gates of the estate.

Panic set in. 'I'll run down,' I said. 'Anton, you go in through the field.' Ylva stayed put on the driveway in case he returned. He had yet to be properly microchipped and had no name tag. He could take off anywhere. 'I've scared the life out of him with my stupidity. He'll be in Cappamore before we get near the gate,' I muttered, running to the gates that we had passed through minutes earlier.

'Don't frighten him, Dara,' Ylva shouted after me as I motored down the hill, the lake now to my left. 'He seems terrified of cattle.' Outside the front gates, I hesitantly took the road to my right that led to the Clare Glens – the famous waterfalls that act as a border between Limerick and Tipperary – passing farms and stand-alone cottages. I then decided to turn and run towards the village, bellowing out Oscar's name as loud as I could, hoping he would recognise my call and forget the cattle that he had just run from. The words, 'Dad, are you there?' echoed out from somewhere behind the eight-foot wall standing beside me. 'What?' I shouted, slowing down, unsure where my son was speaking from. A group of women decked out in sprightly coloured walking apparel began drifting towards me, chatting loudly before politely stepping aside to let me pass as I ran past them in a sweat, but I was far too shaken to salute back at them. They could no doubt see that I was in a panicked state about something or other. It was only when the group had passed me by that I called out, 'Anton?' He instantly replied, 'Over here, Dad.'

'Is Oscar in there?' I called over the wall, searching for a way through. Just then a neighbour waved at me from his garden across the street, pointing a stick in the air, directing me. A 'thank you' was sent in his direction. 'Trying to find the dog,' I shouted back, as a gate finally appeared in front of me. Beyond it was a path to a tiny, forested area from where Anton was calling. He was standing motionless on the forest path. A trail pointed in one direction and a second meandered away in the other. About 500 yards from our new house was a forest I'd had no idea even existed.

'Maybe he's in there somewhere, Anton,' I said, guessing that two trails pointing in opposite directions made something of a loop. It was unlikely to be a large forested area, given that it backed out onto the road from where we had come. I could see it was part of the grounds that we had just been walking through. 'You go that way, I'll go this way,' I said, taking my phone from my pocket to check for any updates. There were none. I then ran along the trail route in something of a circular fashion, left to right. I ran past a small brook, from where it was possible to gaze at the driveway we had come from. The trail led onto another trail, through a small thicket of thorny briars.

I ran in hope that Oscar would reappear. Guilt drove me. Maybe it was my fault he ran away. Why would he return if he sensed he was exposed to harm? I imagined him on his way, finding – in that mysterious sixth sense – a way back to his home. Then a story that was once told to me by my father – about a gun dog that went missing when my grandad was shooting in a bog on a summer's night and that returned to the family home a full three weeks later in mysterious circumstances – entered my consciousness like a dream. I tried to recall the precise details of the story. It was an oracle sent to dampen anxiety. Suddenly, Anton ran past, zooming around the corner waving his hands.

'Stop, Dad,' he said, crashing into my chest. He stumbled to a standstill.

'What is it?' I replied, trying to catch my breath. 'Did you find him?' Anton pointed over at the wall, beyond which was the footpath we had just travelled along to enter the forest, and then further on again would lead to our house.

'Mam said to go back home. I assume she found him.'

'She didn't say?'

I grabbed his shirt sleeve to get his attention, pressing for an answer, surmising that Oscar had been knocked over and Ylva didn't want to tell me by phone. The path took on a new character, large bushes of briars and thorns announcing themselves to my flesh. A child and his mother ran quickly around the corner, gesturing hello to us while passing. A sense of impending disaster brought my leggy walk to a stroll, feet dragging as I said hello in return.

We then stepped through a small inlet – again full of briars – used to enter and exit the forest from the street. My mood darkened further on regaining my breath to push through the opening. We walked in silence at first, glad to have found a forest so close to our home but sensing bad news and using the return journey to prepare for its delivery. I didn't know whether the forest would ever be used as a place to walk a dog now; I didn't know if I even had a dog to walk with. The hedges at the turn home hemmed us in, as the steely white gates of our house appeared. We turned the corner in full. Ylva was waving over at us. She had an upbeat demeanour.

'Come up here,' she declared. 'You're not going to believe where he is.'

'Where?' I said, unable to contain my enthusiasm. I was a bag of nerves.

As Anton and I headed up the drive, the sun pushed through the clouds to form a pink silhouette of sky, the sunset announcing itself as both magical and sublime. My feet began to pick up speed as I lifted my head to survey the parameters of the garden.

At the top of the driveway, I could see the patio transformed into Oscar's bedroom apartment. He was sitting outside, wagging his tail exuberantly at the door. I dropped my phone, the harness and the lead, and ran to him. Embracing his coat, that of a dog assumed to have run away to never return, brought a wave of relief. Sitting motionless in my arms, his stoical pose seemed to usher the words 'not to worry'. As our arms wrapped around him in turns, his demeanour changed, softening with the comforting effect of averted disaster. Ylva had returned home as we went in search of Oscar in the forest. When she arrived, in a dishevelled state, he was there, ears cocked at the door to his room. Whatever had happened, whatever impact the shock had had on him, he had returned home. He had looked up at her, with gentle eyes, suggesting he knew that something was up, before lifting his front paw in a gesture of gratitude. He wanted above all – at least it seemed – to be forgiven for having run off. It felt like he was almost embarrassed by what happened, that his fear of cattle, if this is what propelled him to flee, was something shameful when found in a working sheepdog.

A number of concerns about Oscar's reaction on the Glenstal driveway that afternoon nestled deep within me, especially when it was not possible to ask him, 'Was this what happened?' The first was his ability to change gear, to go from first to fifth in a split second; while we were racing to find him, he must have run home in record time. Then there was the way he crouched down like a tiger stalking his prey after first spotting the cow, instead of ploughing through with his usual verve. On the driveway, he had plunged to the floor, needing to be dragged like a stubborn horse. But no matter how distressed he became, his tail still wagged and his eyes still looked up, so communicative in their expression, as if to say 'It's not me. It's what happened to me in the past.' Sheepdogs like Oscar were often trained on Irish farms to actually herd cattle. But unlike sheep, who kick like the best of them, a 'good belt' from a cow, a kick back of the hind legs at the dog, can have lasting consequences. A dog can die as a result of a blow to the head, or be left so heavily traumatised it effectively ends any chance at a working life. As dog behaviourists explain, trauma at such a young developmental age can be very difficult to overcome.

A few years after that summer evening on the Glenstal drive, we holidayed in a rental cottage close to Easkey in County Sligo. It was Easter. I quickly realised that the boreen (as small roads are known in Ireland) to the sea was so quiet that I could leave the cottage with Oscar off the lead and make it down to the shore in one fell swoop. One day, when caught up listening to music, I became uneasy when there was no sign of Oscar ahead, nor was he lagging behind. I could see the boreen drift ahead, and the stone walls on both sides of the road. The pathway had a smidgeon of grass running up the middle and the stone walls' grey veneer, its speckled moss and lichen growths, seemed to emphasise a void, further exposing the absence of Oscar on the track. I was annoyed at being so totally immersed in music that I took liberties in a place he hardly knew. As usual, going outside his familiar territory was unsettling for him.

I arrived around the corner to find him sitting in the middle of the road, in some kind of silent protest. I clipped the lead on, only to find the act of doing so was in vain. He simply wasn't turning. And then I heard the first loud 'moo' followed by a screeching chorus as the rest of the herd joined in, almost like they were happy verbally bullying a dog clearly scared and vulnerable. *Ah, that again*, I thought to myself, recalling the earlier encounter. He dug his heels in and lurched his head forward, so that my attempt at 'exposure therapy' was cruel and unnecessary. He then began to shiver until I said, 'It's okay, Oscar. We'll just go back.' And then, as soon as we turned back to walk in the other direction, his whole body was suddenly energised like before, as though knowing the problem lay behind us he was happy to remind me of it. He had no intention of passing a field of cattle, perhaps for valid reasons.

The exact reason for running off at Glenstal was never confirmed. Of course, considerable time was taken up speculating on why he had stopped so suddenly in his tracks on the driveway. Quite possibly it was the cow scaring him. Or maybe it was the shock from the fence. But whatever it was, it did not equate (in his eyes) with those who had taken him from the farm and set up camp for him in a new home: our family. This perhaps insignificant observation on my part brought a degree of happiness with it. Yes, I was happy the catastrophe had been averted. But I was also happy that, beyond everything, home was starting to mean something important to Oscar. He trusted enough in us to return home.

Our key takeaway from the ordeal was to speculate on the 'time before'. No matter how much we wanted to discover the truth, we would never be certain of his past life. The next day, I raised the issue with the vet, a quiet man who spoke slowly but always on point. It was Oscar's first appointment and, to travel to the clinic, I had to carry him into the car. When I opened the back door of the car in the middle of Newport village, a small ball of poo fell out in sync with Oscar leaping from the back seat, shivering. The poor guy shat himself. I cleaned the mess up and spent the next few minutes coaxing him into the vet's waiting room. When we finally got in to see the vet, he did a body check, before registering, microchipping and vaccinating Oscar, then feeling for lumps – all the steps towards making him a pet.

The vet opened a file on the clinic computer and discussed the term 'working dog' for Oscar's 'breed' section. More jigsaw pieces fell into place. The vet had specified the breed as collie, but the talk of 'worker' and 'sheepdog' for his file seemed to suggest specifically border collie. More research was required by me. The more I read up on working dogs, the more expansive the category became: guide dogs, sled dogs, hunting and mountain rescue; dogs that guard stuff; sniffer dogs; medical assistance dogs; therapy dogs; herding dogs . . . They were all workers.

Oscar was bred to work livestock – not just sheep but cattle. All kinds of sheepdogs herd. Herding dogs were not just border collies. Kelpies, Australian shepherds and old English sheepdogs also herd and qualify as workers. A rabbit hole was emerging down which I fell. The shenanigans at Glenstal, when Oscar stopped in his tracks before a cow leaning over a fence, took on meaning. Maybe he was originally trained to herd livestock: could he be a cattle dog that had never made the grade? Maybe he was a dog who didn't graduate as was expected. Perhaps something happened that set him off and he was terrified of cattle as a result.

The term 'sheepdog' recalled the haunting loss I had felt reading the prologue to Eileen Battersby's memoir *Ordinary Dogs*. In the book, Battersby tells of her journey through life with her two rescue dogs. The prologue recalls a holiday on a favoured Connemara beach, when a recently deceased sheepdog was discovered by her dogs, in a cave along the seashore, behind a dune. The carcass of the animal drained of life haunts the text, a life other to that of Battersby's own canine companions, who do not have to work for their keep. The discovery of the dead sheepdog alone in a cave is recounted in detail. It is as if the poor creature has found a quiet place to die, unburdened by the seagulls and scavenging birds that fly across the sea throughout the seasons. Describing the visceral bodily decay, Battersby asks, 'Was there an owner searching for him? What kind of life had the dog had? A working life by the look of him; he'd been out in all weather and had earned his keep.' These were similar questions to those that perplexed me, when focusing on the acute difference between a pet and working dog.

Many of my own teenage summers were spent holidaying

in the same Connemara landscape, so different to the other more typically pastoral farming regions of Ireland, so littered with mountain sheep painted with different colourings to distinguish ownership. The same mystical, seductive scenery that comes to life like no other when the sun shines was also harsh and unforgiving in winter, as storms beat in upon the land, not unlike the tornados that redesigned the coastline in some countries. I imagined the working dog Battersby describes in such heartbreaking detail, the Connemara wind pushing driblets of rain into his coat in those final seconds of life. And dying alone, unaccompanied by the farmer who undoubtedly looked after the dog in his way; not a pet, but a dog who works, wedded to the machinery of life fading away across the island.

The life of a sheepdog, like the ghost filtered from Battersby's book, began to obsess me. Why had Oscar quivered in fear that day? Why had he run away? I googled 'working dogs' and 'cattle dogs' while sat in my car outside the vets, and all sorts of hits returned about collies and shepherds, Kelpies and McNabs. But I needed to move. The sun was pushing in through the clouds and the temperatures were becoming un-comfortable. It was not even midday and the thermometer was already reading twenty-four degrees Celsius. I slowly reversed out of the car park and headed for home. Heading off in the direction of the Centra shop on the outskirts of Newport, I approached the turn to Murroe. Just then, cattle appeared, in an echo of the previous evening's outing. It was strange to think that my dog was afraid of cattle. Was Oscar kicked when training to herd? I turned to peer into the back seat at this dog who was slowly coming to embody a much-loved responsibility. I had a real desire to learn about his past, his farm life. 'Oscar,' I said, as he wagged his tail to jump from the car as fast as he could. 'Did you get kicked in the head from a cow? What happened to you in Clare?'

The past was a mystery to solve, an obsession that needled more and more. Going by the vet's inspection that day, Oscar was around four years old at the time I rescued him. That meant four years unknown to me, four years that were an impenetrable blur. The silent protest at Glenstal was a pointer to his pre-us existence, the past pushing through in behavioural characteristics. It was an invitation to speculate about where he came from. He had recoiled in fear at the sight of cattle, making it abundantly clear he was going nowhere near them. He didn't growl or become aggressive in any way; nor did he whimper and cry. Instead, he displayed a remarkable ability to reduce into a lump of mass. His ability to unpack his body of vital forces, to 'play dead' as the posture is known in collie lexicon, was fascinating in itself – and it preceded a web of research around herding dogs that I was soon entangled in.

Then there was his homing instinct: a sheepdog waiting at his patio 'office' while I was frantically running around to find him through a forest, one I didn't know existed.

The forest: *another* discovery of our evening walk.

Spatial orientation is a type of intelligence that never fails to elicit my amazement. It is led by scent. We hadn't even shown Oscar the field at the back of our garden, nor a pathway through the trees, yet he had found his way back in record time. Like a homing pigeon sensing its way, he had shown an innate ability to return to an origin. He ran, scared and perhaps shocked by the fence, through a looped walk of the unknown forest onto a road connecting the estate to another leading from Murroe to Newport.

The former Cambridge scientist, Rupert Sheldrake, has done considerable research into these homing instincts in animals, particularly pigeons but also dogs. Sheldrake describes the homing instinct as one of inexplicable mystery, with stories of dogs travelling hundreds of kilometres to return to their owner. He has also undertaken significant research into dogs who can sense that their owner is returning home, long before the individual in question is even close. The idea that home has meaning within the animal kingdom was fascinating to me; it suggested some deep, almost telepathic connection between physical space and the feeling of comfort and safety associated with the home.

The same intelligence that helped Oscar to survive on a derelict farm for more than six weeks, after possibly being abused, helped him to make his way back home. Some dogs like to hunt, losing themselves in the scents that guide their movements in so many different directions at once – like our family Labrador, whom I had spent hours as a teenager enticing out of parklands when engrossed in the retrieval process. Others, like Oscar, return to their master every time: they run away into the distance in order to circle back to the exact point of origin from where the master instructs.

Oscar's file at the vets stated 'working dog'; 'sheepdog' was an equivalent descriptor. The vet had drawn these conclusions from working in the company of dogs. He logged Oscar as a long-haired black-and-white collie with (dominant and) traditional black-and-white markings. These markings are the most typical for a border collie; symmetrical white lines divide Oscar's face with a full white-collar spread around his neck. Four 'socks' accompany a white sleeve on his right leg. Long-haired black-and-white sheepdog collies like Oscar tend to suffer more than most in hot climates, as the natural terrain for a sheepdog/border collie is the wet and cold mountainous border land between England and Scotland – the border country from, where I now knew for definite, border collies take their name. Smooth-haired dogs were also commonly found across Ireland and the UK. They share the same DNA as their long-haired brethren, but have a smoother and obviously shorter mane.

The popularity of the border collie in Ireland and the UK came largely from the successful TV show *One Man and His Dog* – one of the most-watched series of my childhood – about the trialling escapades of shepherd and dog. The show fed into BBC's rural affairs show *Countryfile*, another dedicated to the British countryside. Like a window into rustic life, *One Man and His Dog* was a monument to farming traditions and herding dogs indigenous to Britain and Ireland, and a show that has enthralled the public on both sides of the Irish Sea for several decades. I began researching border collies and sheepdogs during those first months during a time when borders were in the news, often in reference to the Brexit negotiations or the refugee crisis in Europe. Syria and Greece were front-page business, piquing more considered interest in borders as liminal 'spaces' that divide countries.

Was there any other creature – canine or otherwise – that was named after the border between two nations? Perhaps the Alsatian? But that was in reference to the French region of Alsace that borders Germany, a particular place, as opposed to the border itself. Was there an animal whose very origin was not a nation as such, or a specific site, but the hinterland *between* the two? Was it possible to determine the point of origin for something with a relational form, a place that was neither 'this' nor 'that', a site neither 'here' nor 'there'? Was Oscar akin to a refugee, in search of an origin yet never really at place anywhere?

'Border collie/sheepdog' might have been the breed's name categorising Oscar as a rescue with an estimated age of four, but neither age nor breed was a verifiable fact about his life. These estimates came from a short physical inspection that day. It was possible to get some results through a DNA test, but feeling it was over the top to pay for a less-than-accurate test, I decided to learn about sheepdogs as best I could online. Episodes of *One Man and His Dog* that had been uploaded onto YouTube were my main resource. The TV show's pivotal attraction was the symbioses that form between animals and humans: a team, as opposed to a kind of Darwinian rivalry between organisms. Filming trials in full, the show involves finding the best team. Sheep trialling is a recognised sport, part of farming networks across the world, with competition generally consisting of handlers and dogs, mostly border collies, working a course designed to test their ability.

Some say trialling began in the vast sheep farming traditions of New Zealand, where events evolved as community-orientated activities bringing families together under the behest of the working farm life. In sheepdog trials, the shepherd/handler sends signals to a dog, using whistling sounds and vocals to direct the movement, guiding the dog to track sheep along a designated course. Minor variations of sound enhance the communication; the dog's exceptional sensitivity helping pick up nuances while dutifully concentrating on the task at hand. The dog crouches to 'eye' the sheep, creeps from side to side, moves in circles. For some, 'eye' was crucial; for others, movement. But the combination of 'eye' and movement (discussed as 'bone') is the mark of value.

There are many different trials, with scores based on assorted tasks. It's not just the dog's suitability for the job or the course that gains them points, but the handler's ability to work in tandem with the dog to undertake specific challenges. Activities such as shedding (when the dog is asked to separate the herd in some capacity) or an away drive (when the dog pushes the sheep in a direction that runs counter to their instincts) are good options to include. They are duties that test the team bond. Singling is another of the more difficult tasks the trials are designed to test, where the dog is encouraged to single out a sheep from the herd and bring it to the handler, away from the action. With a set amount of time given to finish the course, the winner isn't determined by who finishes the course in the fastest time. Rather, teams lose points based on faults accrued over the course of the trial – although a designated time exists in which to complete the course. A handler's capacity to work with the dog, my research showed me, was the key. The relationship between the dog and handler, the way they work in tandem, remains, for many, the trial's most important attraction.

It was the suspense of trialling that attracted me to *One Man and His Dog*, the 'will he or won't he' element involved in cheering on a herding team. In some cases, a dog refused, often seen during an away drive. From watching these episodes, I learned about the intricate bond needed between the handler and dog. I understood why the dog reacted to a command. A sense of 'right' and 'wrong' was fostered in a sheepdog – for instance, when it was appropriate to crouch or stand – creating a shared value system resulting from a symbiotic pact. The pact itself, however, does not emerge overnight and does not form with just anyone. It forms with the person felt by the dog to be its master. The more I thought back to when Oscar recoiled in fear on our first evening walk around the Glenstal estate, the more convinced I became that something must have got in the way of the trust between him and his handler. Perhaps Oscar ran away from his original home to the farm I found him in because the trust bond had broken and he was hurt.

This bond is the focus of *Nop's Trials* by Donald McCaig, another of the texts about collies that I consulted in those early days. It is a novel about a sheepdog/border collie called Nop who was stolen from his handler by a rival trialler. Nop is an exceptional stock dog treated well by his handler, Lewis. The book details the bond between Lewis and Nop against the travails of the dog's treatment when stolen. Nop is not merely a worker but a soulmate. The book is celebrated around the world by farmers, agility training lovers and sheepdog/border collie handlers identifying with Lewis, the forlorn, bereft master.

The groomer, John, thought that Oscar, like Nop, would become a great companion, so he must have observed his readiness to trust and foreseen a bond forming between us over time. Maybe Oscar's return from Glenstal was that bond in its early stages of formation. And perhaps him recognising the house as his home was also a sign of his burgeoning integration.

Soon after the evening when Oscar had made his way home from that first aborted walk, something of even greater significance occurred. It was evening and the light was beginning to lose its strength. Darkness was folding upon the day as I ushered Oscar into his one-bedroom patio room. I gently combed his coat in a meticulous fashion. It was now a daily ritual to keep him tidy. It was a chore to coax him into the room, never mind the basket in the patio corner; it was a bed he did not recognise. It had never occurred to me that a dog who had come home with us would not see the bed as his; instead, he was more likely to walk into a room and think the bed was that of another dog. The empty basket was a sad sight. To see him sleeping on cold tiles, like he was forced to face the glacial pinch of life itself, was akin to holding a mirror up to my loss.

It must have been a week after he was brought home that things changed. I tiptoed across the kitchen to see the silhouette of the mountain form through the window. Then I peered in through the window connecting the patio room to the kitchen. With one foot, I nudged the curtains slightly ajar.

I wanted to make as little noise as possible. My look fell upon an unfamiliar scene: Oscar sprawled in his basket. It was a black-and-white mess, his feet pushing forward and back, like a ball of energy in slow motion. I pulled myself back, before gazing in again. Four feet began jerking one way and another, suggesting uneasy sleep. Maybe Oscar was in a dream state, shuffling back and forth as the vision took hold? But what did his vision entail? A past? A future? Some otherworld? But the basket was no longer empty. I looked in upon the scene for a moment, peering in at a sight perhaps wonderful only for me. Then, the picture began to blur and I struggled to grasp details. Salty tears began to fall along my cheeks. It was like watching a pitcher jug of Guinness, slowly settling into a cold glass.

Events that are of very little value for some can be, for others, a source of golden joy. Nothing can prepare us for a bit-by-bit turn from perpetual sadness – that emotion that creeps up upon us over time and stays unwanted – to gradients of joy. Following my father's death, there were months of numb bewilderment, during which a detached sensation pervaded my entire body. Only at certain moments – listening to a song, reading a poem or watching TV – did the force of what had happened the previous summer penetrate the curtains of life. The real punctured through the shutters around my emotions. Pain made its mark as the weight of reality fell upon me – and reality was unwelcome. But as I peeked in through the window at a dog sleeping in a basket, knowing a bed had been found, reality became a sudden source of grace.

Small steps must have preceded the lurch into that basket. Then the moment came upon him: a bed judged to be that of another was now recognised as his own. Trying to picture this event in my mind, the point in time when the object in the room had assumed its intended purpose, brought immense joy. I imagined, conjuring the process in my mind, the move into the basket. The sniffing around the area, sniffing my – by then – affable scent, preceded one paw dipping in. Another followed. Soon a body made itself comfortable in the basket. My mood succumbed to a new web of emotion, perhaps best described as happiness, as I peered in the window at a sleeping dog. It was an echo of all the times previously spent peering into Anton and Karl's room, looking in to see if they were asleep. I must have stared for twenty minutes at the scene. A comfortably sleeping dog was releasing jewels of memory.

Then, a less comfortable memory began to surface: tiptoeing up to the coffin holding my father's body at his wake in Cloondarone. I started to think, peering in at him, of the Holbein masterpiece *The Dead Christ in the Tomb*, painted between 1520 and 1522. I was suspicious of Holbein's intentions in painting the dead Christ, viewing the depicted body as that of an all-too-human idol. In my estimation, something was exceedingly real about the figure of the about-to-rise Christ. Holbein's Christ will indeed rise from the dead, and the shock in seeing the emaciated figure looking so vulnerable and real depicted as such comes from an understanding that Christian faith posits the figure as human and divine. This is the paradox pertaining to Christ, shockingly illuminated by Holbein for the beholder.

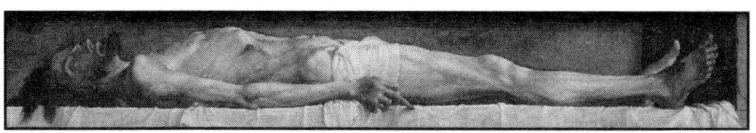

Hans Holbein, *The Dead Christ in the Tomb* (1520–1522)
Kunstmuseum Basel

That same memory led me to the morning of my father's funeral mass, when finishing the eulogy. Thinking about the things my father was drawn to later in life – neighbours dropping by and conversations drifting in different corners – had renewed my thinking about Holbein's Christ. The body in the room next to me during the wake had been battered and bruised like the figure in the painting. At the coffin, I considered formulating a eulogy to 'do justice to him', but the word 'him' was repurposed in the form of absence; it was impossible to process the absence laid out in front of me. I was pushed to consider Holbein's Christ again, as the Christ who will in fact rise. This idea, as a kind of fantasy, stayed with me long after. Perhaps to believe that the dead will rise is a remedy for loss.

Dusk took hold of the room and I was gazing in through the window at a dog gently sleeping. Oscar's body took form as a 'broken' pose, marked by subtle degrees of comfort. Every time a leg jerked up and down, before falling again, a fuzzy, warm sensation permeated my body. It returned me to the lyrics of 'Shelter from the Storm', like a siren directed from the gods. 'I've heard newborn babies wailin' like a mourning dove / And old men with broken teeth stranded without love,' the lyrics advance, the rhetorical ringing, 'do I understand your question man, is it hopeless and forlorn?' The refrain pushes out – '"Come in", she said, "I'll give you shelter from the storm."' To give shelter seemed so right; the storm metaphor so applicable to the Irish weather as it twists from one season to another, and my emotional life. Babies, old men, shelter: words that gathered meaning as a dog slept in a basket. Then the sun disappeared behind the mountains in the distance and bats flew up across the window, swooping from the trees like dabs of paint spattered on sky. I wanted to capture the moment, but there was no point in turning the lights on and waking Oscar up. So I took out my camera to capture the final contours of a sleeping form, before slipping away for the night. The room was transitioning into a dusky afterlife, the sky a full spectrum of blueness.

For six months upon first moving to Murroe, I had walked through the village oblivious to the forest and trail beside it. Whether or not Oscar had run through it during our aborted walk around Glenstal Abbey, the search for him had led Anton and I to terrain that, over the next year, became a second home to me. Irish forests are rare in number. Most have been reclaimed for agricultural land and so Ireland lacks the mass forestry of mainland Europe. Murroe Wood is the name of our address, but if you did not know of the wood behind the eight-foot wall between the abbey and the village, you would struggle to know where the name stems from. Five kilometres north-east of Murroe (on the backroad to Newport in the direction of Rearcross and Upperchurch, and then on to Thurles) was one of Ireland's most impressive forest walks, home to majestic waterfalls on a two-kilometre route: the Clare Glens. From my understanding, Sir Charles Barrington planted thousands of trees during his tenure in the early twentieth century, sourcing tree saplings from all over the world. The forests are thought to have reached as far as the Glens and surrounding territory.

The Glens offered up, no doubt, one of Ireland's most scenic walks and their proximity was a big reason for our settling in Murroe. The trail ascended to a sea of sycamore and cedar, and descended next to one of the most picturesque waterfalls. The walk was both beautiful and terrifying.

Mature trees untypical of the Irish landscape flanked each side. Forests are health and safety concerns in the climate-change era, with storms more prevalent across the island. State councils are bodies accredited to oversee the general preservation of the Glens; trees crashed during storms, yet the route is always open to visitors. On the top of the Glen from the Tipperary side (the falls form a natural border between the counties of Tipperary and Limerick), one could peer over the contours of the Silvermine Mountains. On the Limerick side, the start of the Slieve Felim Way at Glenstal Wood came into view. Ancient forestry is on elevated land. The forest Oscar led me to 500 yards from home may have reached as far as the Glens in the nineteenth century. Populated by deer, foxes, squirrels, owls, bats, pine martens and birds that emit the most vocal song on the island (I learned this from some nature conservationists who travelled from Dublin one Sunday morning), the woods are in very close range. We could walk from home to a forest containing all of these delights of nature.

At the front gates of the abbey, a trail leads along into the forest, running along a kilometre loop. The route is an island within the man-made: the village, monastery, monastery farm, shops, garages, schools and churches. The trail extends from the gate, as if you're entering a distant land of discovery. Tributaries cut up through the forest and someone has turned a ten-metre fallen tree trunk into a seat for kids to congregate at on weekends. Girl guides and scouts meet in balmy summer months when the forest is in bloom and nature is infused with the gush of summer. Another trail crosses a stream, moving up along a path to the monastery. Sometimes, deer are found wandering down from higher ground to feed in this area, munching silently in the woods, stumbling onto the road in the morning – from the opaque wilderness to the urban streets. I found it replenishing to visit the forest in the early morning, to walk or run in whatever season. It was like a prompt that life is like a forest to forage in.

Forests have a longstanding legacy across the arts and human sciences. Writers and artists use the forest to illustrate something essential to the human condition. They are literary metaphors to depict heroic struggle. The beginning of Dante's *Inferno*, as an example, contains – for many scholars – the poem's most arresting lines. 'I found myself within a forest dark,' Dante notes, 'for the straightforward pathway had been lost.' 'Ah me! how hard a thing it is to say,' he advances to 'what was this forest savage, rough, and stern.' Dante paints an image of a sinner seeking the way to God's light. Darkness pervades the forest, but a lack of sun is what makes the forest so threatening a place. For the great Dante, the forest is a symbol of sin; sin feeds on the need for light. Wandering in a forest involves a search for visibility, the sinner grappling in the dark to find the way. In some regards, the forest is a metaphor for the grieving process, when a slip on a stone or a rock at night can leave us tumbling down with no guiding light. But, in daylight, the sensuous sound of birdsong and the engulfing longevity of living trees can be crucial reminders of the life cycle that includes birth. The sun that penetrates through the branches is the hope for better times.

Dante's forest retains its threats. No obvious path out of it exists. One finds, in the savage bent of a wilderness, animals that can and will attack at any given moment. Many of these animals – bears, wolverines and wildcats – have sadly become extinct in Ireland. Those that still reside in twenty-first-century Irish forests tend to live in fear of predatory humans. Many live unobtrusively side by side with human others, rarely making their presence felt. Pine martens, successfully reintroduced to Irish wildlife, thrive in the Glenstal forest where Oscar and I began to habitually walk each morning, but I had yet to see any of these creatures up close. Red squirrels, however, indigenous to the Irish countryside, would appear at any moment, grappling on the trail ground for acorns. I would often notice them scuttle and scamper in lightning-fast time. It was practically impossible to see them close-up.

It was soon after the walk at Glenstal that Oscar and I began to make our way to the forest each morning. Our morning walk was a soon-to-be ritual in the early stages of its formation. The walk or morning stroll took about an hour in total. On our way to the forest, a little gate stood out at the wall situated around the corner from home. Oscar steadfastly pulled on the lead until we were at the gate. Once he had passed through it, he was allowed to run off his lead. We then sauntered in an anti-clockwise direction, trudging around a bend before angling back the other way, the gradient lifting. Passing the bigger trees to our right – the loop nearing its conclusion – Glenstal Abbey stood out in the distance. The presence of walkers on the driveway had a soothing effect on me. It fashioned a sense of camaraderie. I felt part of all that appeared lacking in the greater preserve of forest: the human.

For our first forays in the area, I kept Oscar on his lead to stop him from running off. He would jerk and drag me along, the smell of other dogs luring him like a magnet. He was taken in by scent. Dog walking has altered so much since my teen-age dog-walking days, often spent coaxing a Labrador from a river, her instinct to swim a bane of my life. Hours were also spent trying to find the smaller dog. Whole afternoons were consumed with searching in yellow gorse for a bitch Jack Russell, unfussed by her size in comparison to others. Letting dogs run free, especially medium-sized ones like Oscar, was increasingly difficult in Irish townships. The time when dogs were allowed to wander freely, unbeknownst to their owners, with the kind of independence that often saw them take off for days, to then return hungry, was a distant memory. Laws were passed to inhibit wandering in townships and farmers were more adept at controlling unattended animals in the country with poison.

On those first excursions, Oscar jerked his head back and forth against the lead. As we both gained confidence, he was then given enough licence to run free. He tended to run off around a bend, only to the point at which I would lose sight, then he would hunch and wait, typical of a sheepdog. That he stayed within a limited distance, and always looked for a command, meant it was not long before overconfidence set in. On our fourth morning in the forest, consumed by work

and accustomed to this pattern of running off and waiting – so typical of the trialling I had watched online – I rounded a bend lost in thought. Oscar was gone. I called his name. He did not return. Suddenly I was bellowing his name in the middle of a forest on the edge of the village. Screams and whistles followed, neither of which did anything. I began to run down the trail at speed. I did a full loop, but to no avail. Next, I ran up the middle of the oak-laden area, before taking off down a patch of the woods where teenagers congregate on summer evenings, but he still wasn't there. Then, thinking of our earlier debacle at Glenstal, I sprinted off in the direction of home, all the while trying to maintain a level of calm.

Neighbours were standing together across the street. 'Did you see a black-and-white sheepdog?' I shouted in their direction. A communal 'no' was returned. In panic, still hollering his name, I thought of taking the car in search of him when, for some reason, I returned to the woods through the field adjacent to a pub just behind our house. The briars cut my skin as I kneeled over a hedge that left scrape marks on my hands, before tiptoeing through the soon-to-be-cut grass in front of a thicket of green reconfigured as a boundary. A bar had been repurposed as an entrance for the football and hurling pitch. The bar needed to be pushed over to the side and the briars kicked in before I was launched onto the muddied path that leads on to an old derelict concrete car park. Oscar still didn't appear. I thought again about running back to the gate at the forest opening from where I had just come (from the opposing direction) when my neighbour Davey appeared in my sightline. He was standing on the road, waving his arms in my direction. As my legs pushed on towards where he stood, his stick pointed at the small gate I had just walked through. It was like a scene from a genre action movie. I was the manic detective chasing a criminal to a forest at the edge of town.

I ran up the middle of the road, laughing and crying. Leaping onto the footpath, I then advanced through the gate, shouting 'thank you' in Davey's direction. Inside, like the meaning of a poem had come to me before I had finished reading it, Oscar appeared. He ran over to me, tail wagging at an electric rate, and jumped up, deflating the tension immediately. I tagged his lead on him before turning to Davey who was standing before me. My breathing slowed down in degrees. I stopped.

'I saw him nudge the gate door,' Davey said, as his wife Bridey waved, smiling from across the road.

'I lost sight of him in the woods,' I muttered, more breathless than assumed, before introducing Oscar to Davey.

It was a minor crisis. Yet a friendship with my neighbours began that day. For some years, Davey and his two dogs, Blackie and Prince (who has now sadly passed), would meet us at the forest in the morning. We would talk about all sorts: sport, weather, politics. And the dogs interact like they've been friends since they were pups.

This was the rural community that I had entered so soon after my father's death – six months after he died, to be exact – and that was beginning to open up to me. So much of that first year of grief consisted of adrenaline – of creative bursts of energy mixed with interludes of confusion. And so much of that first year was defined by the fragile and threadbare sheath that linked the present, in the return to rural Ireland and Murroe village, with a past intruding like the ghosts that refuse to be contained in memory vaults. By rescuing Oscar, and rehabilitating him to some degree, I began to forge a deeper reconnection with nature. In the Clare Glens, the sound of gushing water echoed the sea that once regaled my senses as a child. I felt cleansed having completed a circuit. The simple act of walking with Oscar pushing on forward only to return seemed to play on some core belief: the things that go away can and will come back; that, on some fundamental level, it is possible to heal.

The changes in Oscar were also important. His renewed confidence, the joy that awaited me in the morning, offered us new purpose and design. The dog that had bowled me over at the farm, who had brought tears to my eyes as he rested his muzzle underneath the red gate, whining to come back with us, offered up a sign to me: we are not lone figures on a landscape but people who need other beings to survive. The rescue was part rediscovery too; a career in research that coincided with years of urban living, receding to a life more intricately bound to my youth in rural Ireland. In that first year, I was slowly retreading time, rescuing a dog but also resurrecting a part of me I had forgotten existed.

3

Into the Wind

Mishaps continued to occur in the months after that escapade. They mainly came about when Oscar made his way to the woods unaccompanied, strolling down the road to the forest all on his own. Davey rang to say that he had seen him en route. But the roaming soon stopped. As time passed, boundaries strengthened and the walk in the woods solidified itself as our daily ritual. Oscar would run out in front before eventually circling back – and each time he circled back, he looked for affirmation. The outrun and return was a mantra, a rhythm to invoke – perhaps deep in the unconscious – a belief that the things that go away will eventually come back. This mantra became the cycle of life. Oscar's instinct, as such, was to run off only to return to me. Taken as a kind of bond, perhaps a previously unrecognised connection between us, his manoeuvring, which I began to think of as symbiotic, ignited more curiosity again. I set out to gather more information about the dog I was putting my faith in.

Collies, as one of the most common breeds across the island of Ireland, have DNA that can be traced to some of the earliest incarnations of agricultural life on the island itself. One theory traces the Irish collie back to monks who later fled to Scotland. As Gaelic myth illustrates, there was constant traffic of people between Scotland and Ireland. It was, no doubt, the same in the early years of Christianity. The etymology of 'collie' was, in this theory, derived from the old Gaelic word 'coileán', meaning 'pup' or 'dog', thus suggesting that the border collie originates in Ireland. It's also worth noting that in German there is the word 'kuli', which means 'worker', while the English 'coolie' means 'jet black', possibly referencing the dominant colouring of the breed. However, according to some genealogies sourced in Ireland, 'collie' references a companion that helps humans. A coileán was a helper, a pup who is by your side. In modern Irish dictionaries, collie is cited in plural as 'colaí', while in others it appears in the more modern vernacular as the singular 'sípéar' (sheepdog). Perhaps the bond between coileán (or sípéar) and handler was consolidated in centuries past when sheepdogs would spend months in the mountains with handlers. Collies are not single beings in their behaviour but shadows or symbiotic entities. Collie, in addition, is the English vernacular word for a canine type.

Friends ask, 'Is Oscar a collie?' and I hesitate to reply 'yes'. I have no definitive proof. There is no paper stating Oscar is this or that. Going by the vet's analysis, Oscar was best defined as a working sheepdog collie. My research into the heritage of sheepdogs across Ireland and Britain had given me a general understanding of the kind of dog associated with the word 'collie', and a relatively good comprehension of how Oscar's behaviour related to this. The constant looping in the forest began to make sense. The wait at the front door at eight o'clock every morning, pent up with excitement to get going to the forest, was typical behaviour. The crouch and stare, when making his way towards other dogs, began to add up. Oscar's unwavering concentration on an object when moving through wide-open expanses at the back of our house was suddenly clear in purpose. The eyes staring up at me when a bowl was put in his patio, waiting for me to leave before eating, also became apparent in its design.

Although much made sense to me about collie/coileán traits, something about my relationship with Oscar went beyond the specificities or category 'breed'. Something got in the way of the associated criteria. Breeds, after all, are defined by specific traits, but they can fail to encapsulate the plural entanglements around human beings and dogs. If it is true that a big proportion of people anthropomorphise dogs as pets, it is probably also true that certain breeds are more inclined to enter companion relationships with human beings. And one of these breeds is undoubtedly the collie. Maybe – to fully understand Oscar's personality, as I would come to confidently call it – I needed to understand the kind of pact, the dependent states, that collies enter into with other beings.

An anecdote told to me by a friend, when we were both carefree university students, came back to my thinking at this time. My friend returned to Connemara every summer to work at a co-operative of farmers and fishermen outside the village of Roundstone. During those months, one of the farmers regularly came into the shop accompanied by a sheep-dog. The bond was striking. Rope was cast as a temporary lead to keep the dog in check but rarely needed. The sheepdog sat at the door waiting as the farmer passed through the shop for weekly provisions. One Friday, the story went, the work-ers congregated in the pub where it was traditional to mark the end of the week. When the farmer arrived and started drinking excessively at the bar, one of the workers inquired if someone in the village had died. Somebody answered that the farmer's sheepdog had passed.

I thought back to this story, set in a time and place that had enchanted my younger self and that had stuck with me, although the setting was heavily removed from the life I had inhabited at the time. My friend was fascinated by the un-spoken grief that coalesced around the farmer and his dog's sudden absence. Many years later, my mind was a hook, fish-ing in rivers of time, unearthing analogies to help explain the trust evolving between a sheepdog and me.

Like the farmer's dog, Oscar patiently waited for me to return from work. He behaved like his life depended on it, a reminder of the dogs Rupert Sheldrake studied who sensed that their owner, often far away in the city or about to board a train, was travelling home. He stayed at the gate, unperturbed. I returned to a black-and-white form crouched on his stom-ach: another ritual of sorts. As these waiting rites mounted, strengthening our bond that first year together, I began to dwell more on the story told to me so many decades before when I was a student. I pictured the farmer described entering a small rural pub, his head bowed beneath a woollen cap, his wellingtons covering ragged trouser hems. I imagined him edging over to the bar to order his first drink. No words were spoken; a finger was used to order a pint. A drink was served and then the farmer pressed his fingers against the chilled glass. Nothing came from his chapped lips. He sat cradling his drink and then ordered another. An hour passed in the pub while he drank heavily on his own. The pub began to fill up and the farmer worked the room in a drunken state, talking to punters who congregated for the evening. He cut a sullen figure, pacing frantically around the pub with no one to think of but his lonesome self.

The scene stirred my imagination. At no time was the farmer heard to mention his dog, Jess. Diagnosed with cancer, from what I recall, the dog had passed away within weeks. Some of the other farmers knew, but nobody dared to console. I imagined the farmer increasingly drunken, lifting a whiskey glass in the air in salutation before stumbling out the door. The remaining farmers talked about a dog named Jess who travelled with the farmer everywhere. I pictured my friend sitting with his co-workers, taking in an experience that was passed on to me as anecdote. It was a tale that, for some reason, stuck with me. What were the terms of the farmer's grief? Perhaps love was its real source of pain.

I let my imagination roam beyond the pub of the anecdote, following the farmer as he stumbled along a country road that straddled the Connemara village of Roundstone, venturing back into his own sea of absence. He passed a choppy Galway Bay, the crashing waves drowning out his thoughts, a mantra for his newfound loneliness. He walked along the seashore,

stumbling one way and then another, seagulls circling overhead against an elevated moon. Silence was pressing, taking form as nature's music: waves crashing and the wind circulating in the surrounding ether. The farmer kicked seaweed to the side of the road and then stopped to sit for a moment on the rocks leading down to the shore.

He was quiet and still. A small boreen was lit up in the moonlight. He got up from the rocks and shuffled across, as moments of clarity interrupted sustained falling movements. Soon he came to a white cottage with a newly painted door, behind which was a large corrugated shed and a gate where animals can pass through. An old tractor stood idly in the moonlight. He pushed through the door and then on through another, towards a cold bed lying against brick walls. There he slept alone.

Images of the Connemara coastline came to life. It is a landscape where mountains scale to the sea and lakes sparkle in the summer sun. In winter, monumental storms strike the land as the Atlantic rain swirls over the bay, glazing the ground with newly patterned puddles of water. In my imagination, the farmer woke the next day, unsure what had brought on such melancholy, this all-too-pervasive feeling of dread. He dressed and walked out to his biggest field, his beloved Jess no longer by his side. The tracts were not the same; life had changed in an instant. Sheep were still littered across a rocky expanse to the left and a bunch of cattle stood in a small area to his right. Each small herd was once subject to the farmer and his companion Jess in their capacity to move them each day, a team that kept the rhythm of life ticking like a clock.

The anecdote burst to life as a kind of dream: a vision centred on the interdependence of life. The story of a sheepdog brought me to a world where care transmitted in more than one direction, a world where animals and humans coexisted as interdependent, yet a world where most animals were readied for slaughter.

Sheepdogs were called upon to work throughout the day. Livestock was moved, from one pasture to the next, so the dogs had to be ready to jump into action. Cattle or sheep were often moved long distances across difficult terrain and the sheepdog worked long hours to keep the herd in line, to make sure none strayed. Work was a pact between the nonhuman and human. Dogs took form as animal companions, moving livestock that lived in counterpoint to them. But what if the world of farm animals and pets were not exactly separate? What if farm animals lived as domesticated extensions of their companion's self? Perhaps working dogs and pets were equally adept companions, existing as both friends and allies. The human and nonhuman world – this is what struck me when sketching out the life of a lonely bachelor farmer in the corridors of Connemara – was not so naturally opposed. The care a dog returns to its handler played over and over in my mind when contemplating the death of Jess. My farmer grieved the passing of who? Or what? A friend? A person? Hungover and numb, he dug at a hole in the earth. The rain brushed against his eyes, the wind blew his cap this way and that. Clay stuck to an iron shovel. The hole was four feet long. When he finished digging, I imagined the farmer drawing a refuse sack from a wheelbarrow that held the body of Jess, before lowering the carcass into the grave. Rain gushed his face, swirling in a gale; daggers directed from the Atlantic. There were no tears.

The farmer spoke obscenities about paying a vet to dispense with an animal carcass no one wants, content that she was resting in the back field beneath a tree, parallel to larger fields. The hole was mechanically overladen with muck and clay until barely noticeable. The farmer took out a few splintered pieces of wood, tied together in the middle with a piece of rope. He placed the cross at the centre of a little mound, peeking up from the ground. The grave was barely noticeable on the re-laid grass patches, overladen with scratchy parchments of clay on top. Then the farmer knelt down in the mud, his wellingtons stuck in the ground as the rain hit in upon him. Muffled talk – 'in heaven' . . . 'kingdom come' . . . 'daily bread' – brought forth words that would evaporate into the wind.

Around the field, large puddles had begun to form so that shoots of sharp green grass reached up from prisms of rain. The sound of mud being pushed into the ground, as wellingtons squeaked, was met with the human voice. But the farmer was so deep in concentration that the prayer dribbled from his lips like a sacred text, spilling out from the mouth of a Buddhist monk. The prayer flitted through the air, another offering to the gods to dispel the fear of isolation, of human alienation again, listening to the drip from the shed as sleep threatened but never arrived. The human resistance to being alone, to warding off one's own company, was manifest in a sheepdog named Jess, whose body the farmer buried in his field. He was alone again, without her.

And then it was done. The farmer stood up. He walked to a gate; above, grey clouds pushed over the bay and a radiant sun veered out from beneath them. His hands were in his pockets. He climbed the steps beside the gate to return home, where cake and tea were waiting for him. It was his first day alone in fifteen years. It would be months before he mentioned her name, before he drove to Clifden to view a sheepdog pup. He went to a village on the Mayo side of Clifden, where he was ushered through to a small stone shed much like his own, situated at the back of a house. Inside, a thin and beautiful collie bitch stood over a bunch of newly born pups, all of different colours, some even blue and red merle. 'Take your pick,' a farmer said jovially to him, thinking of but not mentioning Jess, as a feisty black-and-white bitch was chosen.

Canine companions have played a role in literature across the ages, from the classic literary texts like *Lassie* to the more recent *Drive Your Plow Over the Bones of the Dead* by Polish Nobel Laureate, Olga Tokarczuk. The latter is a novel and detective story – set at the border between Poland and the Czech Republic, but animal rights is a purposeful tributary running throughout Tokarczuk's murder mystery. The protagonist is a spinster by the name of Janina Duszejko, whose dogs go missing from her home long before Big Foot, her neighbour and a well-known hunter, is found dead by her friend Oddball. Janina suspects murder. She writes to the police authorities to suggest the animals committed 'murder'

as revenge for the hunters deeming them to be subservient beings. As the plot thickens, a priest, Father Rustle, whom Janina challenged over his support of hunting, is found dead. Suspicion intensifies, implicating Janina as a suspect. At this point, the story takes a significant turn, as her missing dogs become the novel's central focus.

Drive Your Plow Over the Bones of the Dead is a strange hymn to the nonhuman. Tokarczuk deconstructs the moral hierarchies of 'nature' that relegate the nonhuman to the shadows of the natural realm. It fictionalises the world to include Janina's non-hierarchical way of seeing. A photograph revealing the murdered priest and others standing over his hunted prey, including Janina's two dogs, takes the form of the textual McGuffin. In the conclusion, the murders are revealed as revenge. The story ends with the anti-heroine fleeing Poland for the Czech Republic, having confessed her crime.

The nonhuman 'other' is the central focus of a novel challenging the reader to apportion a boundary between non-human and human. 'Why is the killing of a deer mere sport, and the killing of a human murder?' asks Sarah Perry in her *Guardian* review of the novel. 'And if animal rights are elevated to those of human rights, would animals then be subject to criminal and human law – if an animal can be said to have been murdered, might it equally be charged with murder? What, moreover, are we for?' Perry challenges us to think of murder in its many forms of manifestation. The novel's world puts the moral quandary of killing others at the core of everyday existence. It is a narrative that confronts the reader with the moral boundaries around animal life: the intimate limit of being itself.

Tokarczuk's message returned my thoughts to the Connemara farmer burying his beloved collie. I sketched it all to question whether it was possible to love the nonhuman. Love *from* the nonhuman animal, many believe, is rooted in our projection. The dog, for example, lifted its paw not because it loved us, but because it anticipated something in return. For the theologian and philosopher St Augustine, love was premised on sacrificing oneself for another being, such as Christ dying for us. But could a nonhuman animal do this for a human? And if not, was it possible for them to 'love' a human? Love of this sacrificial nature, certainly, seemed to drive Janina's passion. Hunting was seen as a cowardly aberration. Maybe I thought of Janina, because as a boy I was integrated into a fox-hunting tradition (since subsequently banned on animal welfare grounds in the UK), hunting regularly with my father on horseback. My grandfather passed on a love of the countryside to my father who encouraged hunting in his children. Or maybe I thought of the novel because it made me dwell on my father as hunter – and someone not unlike those who Janina has problems with.

Some of my fondest memories of my father in later life were from the Saturday mornings when we stayed with him in Cloondarone. The old hunt master, John Pickering, would call in, joined by Loe McDonagh, Dad's neighbour Gabriel Lardner and Mark Killilea, a retired MEP who was one of my father's oldest and dearest friends. (A week after Dad passed away, Mark drove us to the horse sales in Dublin for the sale of Faugheen's half-brother who was being prepped when Dad died. It was a long drive for Mark, who was a diabetic and whose sugar levels dipped as the journey went on, yet he was intent on driving in honour of my father, his lifelong friend.)

The talk at these gatherings was consumed by horses, most often racing but sometimes hunting. The jokes, the banter, the 'craic' as it was known in Ireland were in good supply, and I loved the way my father gathered together such disparate friends, with their love of horses and the country traditions (that Janina Duszejko derides) overriding any class distinction or political difference. Years after his death, I wrote an essay about these spontaneous gatherings that mentioned the song 'When Ye Go Away' by The Waterboys – it was in memory of those ordinary yet so extraordinary gatherings. I remembered the jar of instant coffee (it was quietly unacceptable to have fancy coffee). Perhaps even biscuits. Friends gathered to celebrate the symbiotic culture of keeping animals.

Between the ages of ten and fourteen, I participated in the North Galway Hunt on several occasions. It was, perhaps, my increasing love for our two dogs, Remy and Corey, that eventually made the cruelty involved unpalatable. In my teenage years, I rebelled against a sport widely regarded as an aberration, an opinion I would later come to revise. As a young adult, I began to think again of hunting as placating humanity's animal urges, an outlet for fundamental human aggression. Hunting, I surmised when studying animal ethics in university, unburdened repressed urges, abhorrent to many, while confronting the wild in us all, the tether line between human and animal. To repress, the philosopher in me argued, in the guise of abstracted morality was to sever the human from its primal origins.

I later sourced animal rights studies to put my reasons to the test, including Jonathan Safran Foer's journey into the meat industry in *Eating Animals* and Peter Singer's bible for animal rights activists, *Animal Liberation*. Several of the Welsh philosopher Mark Rowlands's books were more than intriguing points of discussion, in particular his memoir about an eleven-year relationship with a pet wolf called Brenin, *The Philosopher and the Wolf.*

I thought hard about the moral sentiments put forward in these books. The animal husbandry Safran Foer shone a light on was challenging in its descriptive horror, bringing the reader close to the unworldly conditions of the meat-eating industry. I wept at the bond that severs between Rowlands and his companion wolf Brenin when the latter dies, the text born of a love so eloquently described when concerning the final months of Brenin's life. It is probable that these passages, when an ever more reclusive Rowlands and his interspecies pack (Brenin, Nina and Tess) move to the south of France, helped develop my own interest in love in interspecies relationships. As something of an eccentric misanthrope, I also identified with the journey Rowlands describes; the *philia* apportioning to the relationship between human and wolf. As Rowlands suggests, '*philia* – the love appropriate to your pack – is the will to do something for those who are of your pack even though you desperately don't want to do it, even though it horrifies and sickens you, and even though you may have to pay a very high price for it, perhaps heavier than you can bear'.

The Philosopher and the Wolf bore heavily upon me as an influence. So too did my teenage days in pursuit of a fox, another form of *philia*: the intensity of the hunt. I found sentiments echoed in the strangest of places. Roger Scruton was a conservative thinker for whom I had a particular distaste. However, his book on hunting, read when teasing out my thinking, chimed with my memory of the adrenaline rush as I advanced across the countryside of East Clare on my pony, Shadow. There was something intrinsically liberating about human and nonhuman animals blending into the imbroglio of the pack. For Scruton, this was life-enhancing; forcing him to reconsider his whole experience of nature as a result. 'The blood of another species flows through your veins,' he writes of the hunt on horseback, 'stirring the old deposits of collective life, releasing pockets of energy that a million generations laboriously harvested from the crop of human suffering.' At thirteen, I lacked the vocabulary to describe the feelings that Scruton designated here: the hunt as immersion in the now of human and animal existence that somehow, against the protestations, seemed right. I would later recalibrate this view – as in, I would later become less sympathetic to hunting.

One of the more difficult animal rights-based studies, *Zoopolis* by Sue Donaldson and Will Kymlicka, made me think specifically about pets. In the book, a theory of nonhuman citizenship is proposed. Animals, from the domestic to wild, are explored around the idea of 'flourishing' as the manifest form of a sentient life. The extent to which an animal flourishes according to a species norm, a manner of being in the wild or in a specific social context is one of the text's pivoting concerns. An example is a swift and its migratory patterns, or a squirrel foraging for acorns in the wild, or a sheepdog whose prey drive remains active when the act of killing is reoriented into herding sheep.

This concern with norms brought about something of a moral quandary. It begged the question of how we can know the instinctual needs of a nonhuman to help them to flourish at a job. As I made my way through dense passages of text, 'flourishing' needled as a concept. My desire for Oscar to flourish in the mode described by the authors was really a desire to explore personhood. *Zoopolis* is not a book for everyone's tastes, but it did reveal a non-hierarchical relationship between humans and nonhumans that was most applicable to the non-hierarchic relationship I initiated between Oscar and myself. I was particularly uncomfortable with the kind of bow-down authority a lot of the sites dedicated to keeping pets seemed to advocate as best practice. I wanted Oscar to come to me because he wanted to come to me, not because I was ordering him to or because I was feeding him with tasty canine treats.

Keeping pets like prisoners bothered me as a teenager, given that my father had an Irish horse farm that involved stabling horses. He built stables at the back of our house, while the farm itself lay a few kilometres from Tuam, in that hinterland between the urban and the rural. Farmers and members of the travelling community were those who formed lasting relationships with domestic animals, sharing labour and activity. Those same fox hunters were the ones investing time, nurturing animals in differing capacities, unlike the protesters

I saw criticising the sport from urban settings. Many farmers understood themselves as part of a greater ecosystem.

And, yet, moral concerns brewed up when fox blood was painted on my face. 'Blooding', as it is known widely in hunting circles, is an ancient practice that was used to mark a participant's first experience of a kill. This was usually the youngest member of the hunt, singled out for the initiation ritual. In one regard, the child is accepted by the initiated, buoyed by the significance of the event. On the other, the moral issue of killing is seen as an acceptable treatment of animals.

To one degree or another, these moral concerns around working relationships with animals bubbled over in my relationship with Oscar. Every morning, he waited, his body a clock that pulsated on the chime of 8 a.m., that time before work when domestic duties were fulfilled and we could be together, a daily habit that helped me re-evaluate the essence of animal–human relations. Maybe the truth was the changing 'relations' – the slippery border point where one organism dissolved into another.

The US feminist philosopher Donna J. Haraway and the British nature writer and bestselling author of *H is For Hawk*, Helen Macdonald, both explore such relations between human and nonhuman. Haraway writes about the synergy between dogs and humans in *The Companion Species Manifesto*; Macdonald is specially drawn towards birds, or ornithology. 'Telling a story of co-habitation, co-evolution, and embodied cross-species sociality,' Haraway notes, 'the present manifesto asks which of two cobbled together figures – cyborgs and companion species – might more fruitfully inform liveable politics and ontologies in current life worlds.' Haraway's emphasis is 'companionship', a canine–human criterion that compels us to record stories of care. Macdonald, on the other hand, focuses on the wild, near-untameable bird of prey, the goshawk. After the loss of her father, Macdonald sought solace in the hawk's 'otherness'. The training endeavour, a rollercoaster of emotion knitted into the behaviours of a wild creature, reads like a thriller. Macdonald's descent into the subculture of hawkery, with all its attendant obsessions, and her desire for a kernel of recognition is, I feel, an attempt to maintain a living connection with the deceased.

Macdonald's fascination with the goshawk – expressed in her expansive and descriptive prose about the intricacies of the wild – lies, in part, in the beauty of the hunt itself. Sheepdog aesthetics, in contrast to this, are defined by the bending-back of a prey drive as a type of symbiosis: transforming the kill – via the intervention of humankind – into care. There is an equally alluring beauty to the entanglement of nature and culture as nature-culture, to draw from Haraway's many concepts. The handler stands, sometimes with a whistle hanging from their mouth, like a *plein air* painter with a brush, the canvas taking form as a black-and-white movement across the field. Bred to be part of the orchestra of rural life, sheepdogs coexist in a continuum that, as time changes and the ways of the land change with it, sees many canine creatures left behind, like old musical instruments left hanging on a wall.

An animal rescue industry took root in rural Ireland around the problem of abandoned sheepdogs, some of whom never made it as workers. Others are the excess of dramatic change in country practices. High energy and neurotic personalities are a difficult sell to urban households. In addition, there is little access to the agility sports these animals require to stay active – and as advocated by Haraway. It is not a coincidence that the dogs who excel in agility competitions are sheepdogs of a sort, most notably border collies. Haraway writes about the merino sheep farming tradition in the state where the agility competitions she takes part in with her Australian shepherd Mr Cayenne Pepper are held. Focus is given to the pair's interactions when undertaking the activities that enable the dog to work as a companion animal. Both undergo a co-evolution that comes about from the dog flourishing as a working partner, from transforming the prey drive. Agility gives the dog and handler purpose, like sheep trialling. It is a physical activity based on trust and collaboration.

A black-and-white body runs into the light, a silhouette disappearing into foliage melting from green to brown. It is mucky and wet in the forest, even in summer. Oscar appears from nowhere – tongue out, ears propped in anticipation of command. We are two in the form of one. As summer turned to autumn and morning walks turned to excursions at sunrise, other things turned too. Oscar fell in love with the car, lying in it for hours on end. Our relationship entered a new season. Things I had at first barely noticed about him began to strike me as unique: a refusal to eat until everyone was in bed, a glassy-eyed stare in my direction when leaving his bowl. His little quirks intrigued me. When I emerged in the morning, a shuffling came from the patio, Oscar having held in his toilet needs overnight. Once he was out, he wiggled his backside and stood on his hind legs, as I waited at the door entranced. Then, as he burst in and out again, he made straight for the bushes, relieved himself and then, like an arrow hurtling towards me, appeared to unpack the words 'I'm back'. There was no way he would even contemplate going anywhere without me. The moving objects that so commanded the instincts of typical sheepdogs, some of whom were so obsessed with balls and Frisbee that they slept with them at night, was of little interest to him. All he wanted was to be by my side.

And so, as the days mounted up, each morning was a reminder that we were bound together. I sought to understand more and more about him: his exuberance when the lead was pulled from my pocket in the morning, dancing along the driveway to the road, sometimes standing on his hind legs or running in circles. He was so enthused by the prospect of visiting the woods, I began to film and post the videos – his pre-walk ritual, that wiggling dance – to an online border collie/sheepdog forum I joined on Facebook. Over time, as our connection strengthened, my posts began to gather a wider audience, from Melbourne in Australia, to Portland, Oregon in the US, to Carmarthen in Wales.

As I initially posted the videos simply to gather feedback, to learn about Oscar's specific breeding, I was more than taken aback when members wrote to say that Oscar reminded them of their beloved border collies who passed years before.

One woman inquired about coming to visit Oscar when she was in Europe; to hold such a friendly and serene dog, she commented, would be akin to swimming with dolphins. She wrote about her long-lost dog, Mia. Mia shepherded her through her husband's lengthy battle with cancer, waiting at the door every day for her return from the hospice, her eyes looking up to say, 'I know'. Another forum member, an elderly retiree living in California, wrote to me about a collie that appeared on the side of a road one evening when he was patrolling the highways. Like the imagined farmer mourning his beloved Jess, the man spoke of his beloved Yogi. His collie was a long-lost child, a spirit who had descended upon him in his greatest hour of need.

The border collie/sheepdog forum consisted of all types: urban dwellers who had taken on the challenge of keeping a city collie, juggling work with the required windows of time needed to exercise their dog; mountain rescuers who had taken a work partner home as a retiree; buck ranchers who liked to watch their sheepdog run free in the open spaces of the prairie. Farmers who had sourced a border collie puppy for herding work on a farm often found the same dog became, over time, a deep companion of the heart. There were so many uplifting stories on the forum, so many helpful insights into the breed. Oscar's rush of excitement when a walk beckoned was pretty much, I came to think, the surge that exhilarates a working dog when put to the test.

Border collie sheepdogs are widely considered to form robust bonds with handlers. It was not unusual to find a dog and its handler playing in a park, the dog fixated – to a point of obsession – on a Frisbee. Other canine breeds would look to distract and play, but collies had little interest in recreation once their mind was set on an object – and therefore a job. So many collies were returned to dog pounds for rehoming because an owner who had not done their research was put off by the dog following them around the house, staring at them. This was normal stuff that unsettled them. People were put off by the 'eye' continuously gazing up in their direction, waiting on the command signal.

All this meant that collies needed constant stimulation. Some chased all day, bereft of an off switch; they then fell into a physical stupor, suffering 'border collie collapse'. But mental – as much as physical – stimulation was vital, along with a sense that the dog was fulfilling its purpose. Although Oscar was capable of sustained concentrated movement, eyeballing a squirrel at a distance before making his move, he would often veer off in the opposite direction of congregations of people and their dogs at parks, beaches or fields. He would then sit staring at them from the one obvious exit. In this, I felt his purpose was to guard, to watch over, to make sure none of the group broke off to start doing their own thing. And this made me think that he viewed our family in a similar way, his job being to wait in case of any sudden movement that might break up the herd. He became, in this sense, a kind of family Superglue, his function being to bond us all together. This intrigued me. Perhaps Oscar's wiggling morning shuffle expressed joy in this regard, looking forward to a day doing what he was bred for: to look over us in the depths of nature. His desire to be with me, his instinct to run the outreach in a pear-shaped route before returning safely, was a trait I rarely encountered with the dogs we had in my teens. On the contrary, I spent whole afternoons wading through the marshes of Tuam's palace grounds in search of a Labrador taken in the direction of game, trying to retrieve prey in the wild. Countless more afternoons were consumed crawling through bushes and over ivy-adorned walls in search of a terrier who barked incessantly when immersed in an activity approximating a hunt. It was nice that these dogs were led by instinct to seek and search. But there was something about Oscar's instinct to return to me, something about his coming into my life when he did, that I could not explain. And perhaps, on some deeper spiritual level, he came into my life for a reason. I wanted to know why.

I stumbled on to the work of philosopher-poet Denise Riley around this time. When Riley's adult son Jacob unexpectedly died of a heart attack in Spain, his death brought upon her a shattering grief. After years trying to process her loss, Riley wrote an essay and poetry book about Jacob. The book, *Say Something Back*, was adjoined with an essay, 'Time Lived Without Its Flow'. In both texts, Riley explores grief as an altered experience of time. 'Hard to put into words, yet absolutely lucid as you inhabit it daily,' the author writes, 'this sensation of having been lifted clean out of habitual time only becomes a trial if you attempt to make it intelligible to those who've not experienced it.'

A persistent symptom around her loss, Riley noted, was the difficulty in projecting oneself into the future. One felt stranded in time. One's thinking was overladen with memory. The mechanics of flow break down. In addition, Riley found it difficult to describe her loss to others. Atemporality was hard to articulate, a problem she came to regard as a kind of reckoning with the limitations of language. 'I want to try, however much against the odds,' Riley writes, 'to convey only the one striking aspect: this curious sense of being pulled right outside of time, as if beached in a clear light.' I found in this sentence a solace of sorts. That first year after Dad passed away, I felt the same beached sensation. Life was a struggle; lifting myself to do things was hard. Simple activities took up so much energy: going to the shop, driving to work, mowing the lawn, even just grabbing the mail from the letterbox. Every new task seemed to demand more looking outwards, more of my much-conserved energy.

And so the pendulum swung, and life went on, all the while, like Riley's, devoid of the spurts of ecstatic energy that were needed to make life really meaningful again. The lights dimmed, as one person said to me, and every once-cherished activity became a chore. Meeting with friends felt like a good thing to do, but then sitting in a group as everyone laughed and talked of upcoming events made me want to jump up and go home. By walking the ancient pathways with Oscar, each step on the land, each hour walked was a plea to a distant future. Apart from spending time with him, Oscar asked very little of me. And somehow, by simplifying life's equations, he staved off the real cause of loss: loneliness.

'I need a crowd of people,' Neil Young sang on his sadly beautiful 'On the Beach', 'but I can't face them day to day.' Young's lyric was a striking invocation of the paradoxical in grief: it did not make sense.

Sixteen months had passed. Grief advanced from the kind of shock Riley writes of to the heaviness of loss, a weightiness of the senses. As the seasons changed and walking in the forest with Oscar strengthened as a habit, everything in the phenomenological world seemed to drag me back to the past. I existed with both feet in the past. The future was an extravagant luxury I was trying my best to map my desire onto.

My experience of loss unleashed a kind of fantasy that was made manifest at this time; that a higher power was orchestrating things from another world and that my father had brought Oscar to shepherd me, to cushion his own absence. The rhetorical question of 'Where have you gone?' brought answers I retrospectively – and perhaps with the help of Riley's texts – looked upon as a kind of denial. My father, as the Irish adage went, was looking down from above. Falling upon this fantasy maintained a belief that death itself was not an end. In fact, the person whose number was still on my phone, whose wallet was still in my locker, whose possessions were scattered in my garage, was merely gone. Grief was knowing someone had died while acting like they were alive, just elsewhere.

Maybe it was more that I accepted 'he's gone' but could not process the 'gone for ever' bit. To know but not feel the repercussions of loss was the condition Riley elaborated on ('knowing and also not knowing that he's dead. Or I "know" it but privately I can't feel it to be so') in detail. Slow to call it 'denial', it was nonetheless best filed in the category of denial. Riley had evidence to prove Jacob's death but expected his return: what went away must come back. She struggled to compute the meaning of the word 'gone' and sought support while trying to write and grappling with the idea of being there for a son who was suddenly not there. The same acceptance and disbelief informed my fantasy. I fantasised that Oscar would release me into the future. He came to me for a reason. That is, my loss was not mine. It was shared with the spirit of the dead.

In the years leading up to his death, my father took to walking Knockma, known as Castlehacket to locals, on a daily basis. Close to Cloondarone, Knockma is a site of Irish folklore. It is regarded as the resting place of Queen Medbh ('Maeve' in English) who once ruled Connacht, the western province of Ireland, long before the arrival of Christianity. Medbh was the quintessential mythological Irish heroine, most famous for her part in the Irish epic *Táin Bó Cúailnge*, known as 'The Cattle Raid of Cooley', the story of a famous raid north to steal a bull. I was told this story as a child by some relation, perhaps an uncle, on one of my first excursions to Knockma. Faeries, cairns and all the other riches of folklore as told orally were encased in this site, one so easily forgotten in the throes of modern life.

Today, Knockma is a trail made up of looped walks offering panoramic views of north Galway and Mayo – the wetlands of Caherlistrane and Corofin, the vast fields of grazing sheep, the peaks of the western seaboard. Even when my father was sixty-plus in age, we would walk the steeper anticlockwise route together, his feet having improved enough to travel unimpaired. Never one to amble, preferring to walk for practical reasons, he was forever drawn to the more hair-raising stuff. But this late period was memorable for our slower pace: the chat while getting the steps in and being in company. Yet it was still hard to square the memory of these walks with the 'gone for ever' bit in the loss equation.

For Dad and I, the pace was slowing, but for Oscar and I, it was increasing. Our morning walks soon turned into runs, an activity that I had all but stopped in middle age. I soon came to cherish running with a dog by my side (especially one that takes off into the distance before circling back to me) and running reduced the time needed to keep a collie active. Mountain trails became our main sources of activity. The Slieve Felim Way was a retreat from the daily grind, but it was more than a breathtaking route through mountains. The Way was for many, and still is, a spiritual undertaking in rough terrain. I was told that it was one of the country's oldest pilgrimages and that our ancestors once walked it, into ancient light. The suspected pilgrimage began from the point where we started our run – on the fringes of Murroe. From there, a small ascent moved west, pushing along hilly terrain towards the village of Toor. The trail then circled back towards Keeper Hill and on to the Silvermines.

The route is through an eerie landscape. For the first few kilometres, forested sections receded into outbursts of scree, marking the higher planes. I was able to gaze out over the countryside from an elevated position. The pilgrimage, forty-three kilometres in length, took upwards of ten hours to complete on foot. I began walking sections of the route,

but was soon running it with Oscar. Greater distances were soon manageable and, within weeks, I was comfortably running for an hour. Some days, we began at the car park in the woods and made our way to a plateau about three kilometres in. After two further kilometres, at the scree we would turn for home. From a height, I could peer over the valleys at the farmed Tipperary grasslands below and a God's eye view of bungalows, dotted white specks on a carpet of green, was proffered from the mountain range.

The return was all downhill. Running side by side on the way back to the car, the profile of animal and human reached a rhythmic synchronicity of being. All the pent-up adrenaline pushing through me from one day to the next relented into the wind. As we ran, I took the opportunity to shout out into the vacuum of the mountain range, as a lone cuckoo called out in reply. I would shout, but Oscar was quiet. He never barked.

One Saturday in the spring of 2018, Ylva and I were hiking the signposted Discover Ireland route along the Slieve Felim when the road forked in two directions. A purple sign pointed to the circuit from the car park starting point, while a second sign indicated a pathway drifting down the mountain to some unknown destination. The completely barren land was marked by quite rugged topography, with culled trees giving the impression of a post-apocalyptic scene taken from a sci-fi B-movie. Oscar ran along an incline, passing tree stumps rotting in a man-altered landscape. Then he suddenly took off in another direction, sprinting with all the speed he could muster. He shifted gears alarmingly. A light seemed to have turned on in his brain; it was like a spell had been cast upon him. His silhouette disappeared over the horizon, dissolving into fog. In that moment, the degree to which I had come to lean on him revealed itself in full.

I looked at Ylva.

'What will I do? Just stay here?'

I couldn't. I dropped my bag and stick, sprinting along the boreen adjacent to the field Oscar had just run through, leaving Ylva behind. I heard her whistle, using two fingers to sound out a screeching noise he had become accustomed to. A spate of recently culled trees led down towards a distant abyss before which my body faltered to an anxious standstill. My dog seemed to have vanished into thin air.

Panic began to rise. But then, on a path that seemed to thread its way through the mountain, the story my father had once told me as a child about my grandad shooting in a bog on the border between Galway and Mayo rushed to consciousness again, this time full of all the minute detail it was lacking before. Darkness was falling. Grandad was deep in concentration, his German pointer sitting by his side. On the horizon was a light which, unsure where his car was parked, he made his way towards. It grew further away as he walked, but at last a cottage came into view. He knocked on the door and an elderly woman answered. She shone a light over my grandfather, at which point his dog just ran off into the dark. Grandad called out the dog's name, but he was nowhere to be found. Taking refuge for a few hours (it was the custom then to open your door to strangers in need), he had tea and cake with the lady before setting out to find his dog in the night. Hours were spent searching, but his beloved dog was nowhere to be found. My grandfather made it home several kilometres to Tuam that night, consumed with real sadness.

Weeks later, whimpering noises were heard coming from the front of the house. The whimpering was soon joined by scratching. Dr Tony Waldron made his way to the front door to see if someone was knocking. At the door, a dog covered in muck stared up at him, tail wagging. The dog had reached his holy grail. The pointer went on to stay by my grandfather's side for many years to come. I thought of this story, panic-stricken, staring at shadows, while trying to grasp the intention of the animal other, of Oscar. Perhaps I would have to walk unknown roads that evening and maybe that night too, across hills and gullies never imagined, in search of a creature that had – over time – become a crutch; a 'person' to lean upon when facing the day.

On the mountain road that afternoon, the name 'Oscar, Oscar' rang out. But I was also standing in the past, in my grandfather's home, recalling the first hearing of that story from my recently deceased father. The mystery of the Irish countryside was instilled in me at a young age through that oral tradition. My memory of Knockma and the tales of Queen Medbh that seemed to carry me into the bosom of Ireland as a child coexisted with memories of lying in bed as a schoolkid, with my uncle or my father telling me about the magical countryside. These tales of old forged a sense of belonging that I had tried to replicate with my own children, though it was hard to do so in the internet and screen age. That day, however, on the Slieve Felim, I thought of the pointer returning home, galloping through the fields, and how much the tale, whether I remembered it in full or imagined certain details of it, had meant to my dad, who had witnessed the apparent 'miracle'. Now the account came to life, like a transmission from one age to another, a missive of time that refreshed itself anew, as all the great narratives and myths of our time have done. Oscar was the pointer of old and I had become my grandfather, standing in his shoes, as time collapsed upon itself.

I began to make my way back up the road, dwelling on the disappearance. Perhaps there really was no one looking down from above. Panic in the mountains struck at the heart of the belief that Oscar was sent to shepherd me, that he'd come to mind me. Perhaps the story was a way of holding on to a misconceived belief in death as a passage to another place. I pictured myself shouting his name from a window, posting a photo on Facebook: Oscar was missing in the Silvermines. But my grandfather was at the table, a cup of tea in his hand, children shouting and screaming upstairs, the front door opening and closing. Sick patients were waiting to see him; the hum of activity that allows only for moments of rest. The slow drone of a wireless stationed above the presses by the inner wall. Grandad, a man I came to cherish, heard the whelp, the scratch from the front door of the house. He got up, spilling tea on the table. He cursed aloud. He was too tired to be excited. He picked up his cane and made his way to the front of the house, passing riding boots and horsewhips on the way. The door beckoned. He slowly opened it to see a pointer stare at him before he was pushed back upon his bad hip.

I was on a boreen, my father whispering the denouement of the story. My heart was empty and Oscar was lost. Squatting to draw breath, I sucked the air. I started to trudge up the hill like a soldier arriving home from the front, legs beginning to slow. Then came an oasis in the form of a human smile. I sprinted towards it. Relief came quickly. My wife was holding Oscar in her arms. Thrusting my face into her bosom, I cried.

'He's okay,' she whispered. 'I tried to phone you, but I couldn't get a signal up here.'

My panting breath condensed like smoke from a chimney. We huddled and the mood stabilised – he had come back again. A poor phone signal was all it took to suggest catastrophe on the trail. And the same poor signal had made the penny drop. If something had happened to Oscar, maybe my world would fall apart. There was something of my father's ethereal presence in his being.

'How did you find him?' I said, still in shock.

'When you ran down after him, I stayed here,' Ylva explained, standing up from a squat. 'He appeared over there.' She pointed at the culled trees. 'He took off on the road you went after him on, before circling back.'

'Oscar,' I announced, grabbing his hips and pushing my head to brush against his wagging tail, 'you nearly frightened us to death.'

It was the one time that he did something out of character on a hike, the one time he took off with such defining gusto. A suitable cause offered itself in due course: deer scent. Deer leave a powerful odour in mountainous regions, often generating such bizarre reflexes in dogs that it propels them into a frenzy. The typical herding dog mannerisms – the crouching, the staring, the creeping in slow motion – were, of course, those of the instinctual hunter. But in herding dogs, the prey instinct, the final phase in the hunt, was usually turned in on itself. To witness this transformed instinct was to watch a nonhuman animal working in symbiosis with man. It was to watch nature bent to human ends – culture in its fullest form of expression. Hiking in the Slieve Felim that Saturday, Oscar the hunter made a momentary reappearance in our life – until he heard the whistle from Ylva. The call intervened and a sheepdog returned. He gave up on the prey and he returned to the arms of his dearest mistress.

Along with deer scent, sheepdogs are sensitive to sound. They are not hunting dogs, attuned to gunshot; sustained banging causes distress. They suffer more than most from fireworks. Some nights, Oscar became so animated he would pace up and down the garden, distressed beyond measure. He was a crazed automaton. On one occasion, he jumped the hedge in the manner of a Grand National horse – something he would never do in normal circumstances. At first, I thought it was simply fireworks causing these episodes, but it soon became apparent to me that it was a sort of fit. The only way I could calm Oscar down was to coax him into the car and drive around for a duration of time. It often took around thirty minutes to calm him. He would hunch behind my seat, while I rubbed him gently with my hand from the driver's seat and whispered to him. One time, it took driving all the way to a roundabout on the outskirts of

Limerick city, at least twenty minutes at full speed, to calm him down. Then, at some point on the return journey, he jumped up onto the back seat, signalling the end of the episode. Once home, I watched him saunter into his bed like nothing untoward had just occurred.

My amateur diagnosis was epilepsy: he needed medication. But the episodes weren't seizures. He was lucid. After a time, he snapped out and returned to normal. I turned to various online forums to inquire what was causing the fits before the realisation arrived: Oscar has the canine equivalent of panic attacks. That the episodes tended to occur at night indicated a deeper connection to the vagaries of his past life, to all those nights spent alone on the farm, separated from human company. That the car journey tended to soothe him back to himself was also suggestive. It was a car journey that had saved him from his life alone on the farm – on that summer evening when he came home with us.

Oscar, not unusually for a collie, had separation anxiety. Being alone was not his natural disposition. A theory of evolution based on survival of the fittest ran contrary to my experience of companionship: the conceptual coileán as canine helper to Gaelic brethren. In 1869, when responding to Darwin's theory, the Swiss botanist Simon Schwendener registered the 'dual hypothesis of lichens' theory from which the term symbiosis came. The idea that two organisms living side by side might find nutrients to enhance each other's survival was rejected; it was regarded as a dominating relationship. Schwendener was attacked by establishment taxonomists and by scientists intent on making the order of things run in a particular way. The consensus, qua Darwin, was that a species comes to fruition through phases of evolutionary divergence. As a result, theories of pacts that operate in modes of convergence and partners were inevitably sidelined. More than a century on from this, a view of nature as the realm of mutually beneficial 'symbioses' has become widely accepted. Schwendener's hypothesis is now seen as fact.

Symbiosis intrigued me as a concept; not because it suggested that organisms coexist, but because it totally upended the master–slave relationship so impactful on philosophy too. The important thing to note, the crucial thing for me, was that these organisms are not in fact singular entities: their very existence is a coexistence. My relationship with Oscar was symbiotic, in that I took the nutrients I needed – the pull out into the fresh air – which he also took of me: two-beings-as-one.

Oscar panicked at night and, from my cursory understanding, from durations of time when we were away and he was left alone uninterrupted on his patio, or when the usual order of the day was askew. CBD oil was suggested to soothe him, but I decided against it. The occasional drive to the roundabout late at night was the price of love. At times, the crutch had to be transferred in a different direction. In all truth, it was comforting for me to find, in my dog, traits not so different to my own. For I too tended to panic when alone. I too have struggled, throughout life, with the condition of being as one.

That pleasure in being with Oscar in relative silence (the

one that becomes two) was difficult to explain. But it always had a soothing impact on me. The night drives – as music played in the background, with Oscar huddled in the space between the back and front seat, triggered by something I was unable to ask him about – were the instalments of care that I took on as the burden of our responsibility. So much has been written over the years about dogs as pack creatures, their natural state as multiplicity, which undoubtedly has merit. But where the pack was not possible, a partnership sufficed. In the countryside near our home, path lines were weaved through the mountains, along roads where cattle and sheep were once driven by 'drovers', the handlers who spent long days with a dog by their side helping to deliver livestock from one end of the county to another. The cool air of outside – as handler and dog worked in unison, moving through the quickly changing terrain – was so different to the walled-in experience of being alone, which itself was so akin to solitary confinement. Loneliness was for Oscar – as for so many humans whose voices remain unheard today – the price of modern living, an unwanted existence of isolation. As for so many, panic was the physical response to isolation.

Storms, as well as fireworks, triggered Oscar. Collies in general are super-responsive to the rhythms of the world, to the music of the earth – and storms are terrifying for most of their kind. Oscar's sensitivity to sound was such that minor changes in my tone of voice could overwhelm his mood, sending him from joyous attention to sad submission. Sometimes, when his name was called from the back door, his head would bob up in the wild grass of the back field – beyond the boundary I had set for him, which falls at the end of the garden. His ears pricked up as he began making his way back along a well-worn path through the trees. I often bellowed out a loud disciplinary 'no', while pointing firmly at the field, in a further attempt at boundary training (although, at this point, it was akin to telling off a child whose face is already smothered in ice cream and who is holding a tub from the freezer). Oscar's forward trot froze in motion. His whole demeanour would then alter in response to my voice, crouching on his tummy, pushing his face against the grass. A sudden change in manner – from bold to obedient.

My plan was to film this sequence of movement – through the fields and bushes home – to show to a dog behavourist who had befriended me through an online collie forum. Once the footage was posted, he very quickly messaged to say that he had watched the clip and that the skills of a highly bred working sheepdog could be detected in Oscar's behaviour. Oscar demonstrated, he told me in no uncertain terms, herding traits. He reacted to tonal variation and he behaved accordingly. His susceptibility to sound and his incredible ability to feel emotion was from a longstanding genealogical heritage of breeding and training: culture-nature. Try as much as you might to scold him, his sensitivity to a raised voice made it hard to do so. He would look at you as if you were scolding his being. It was like he was suffering from having failed you. Perhaps this was part of his lineage, part of his gentle nature, from being raised in the quiet of the country. Or maybe it was tied to events of his past.

That the world contained such respondent creatures, creatures so fully cognisant and at times ashamed of their behaviour, was more than intriguing. One forum member replied to my posts, noting that 'He lives for you. You can see that his whole "job", as they say, is his service. You're his master now.' It was a nice comment for several reasons, not least in the pleasure taken from being thought of as a dog's master. But, after analysis, it also brought a degree of guilt on my part in the references to his job and service. It begged a question: what was Oscar's 'job' now? With me? I worried that Oscar was not 'flourishing' as a 'sheepdog', that he was lacking in purpose. I was uneasy that he had been retired from work before his time. Sheepdogs, so symbiotic in their essence, need purpose. And I really needed to know more about Oscar's lineage and heritage. Did herding extend to guarding? Sheepdogs are generally kept in check, in sheds or farmhouses in modern times. But, in decades past, they spent days alone with a shepherd, guarding flock as they passed in droves along pathways linking regions together.

Oscar's herding instincts came to the fore when we holidayed in the village of Enniscrone in County Sligo at Easter 2018. I felt excitement and unease in equal measure about bringing Oscar on the trip, his first real holiday as part of the family after nearly a year living with us. Sheepdogs are such routine-based animals; they get anxious about any kind of change. We had planned for Oscar to stay in our cottage with us, even though – by habitual inclination – he was an outside dog. Bringing him along meant I would have to take him for a long walk on the beach every morning so he would settle in the house during the daytime. As a seaside village, Enniscrone's main street runs parallel to one of Ireland's widest beaches. It is a surfing haven with a five-kilometre strand. To get to the beach, you walk past a row of terraced cottages, parallel to which is a river that flows into the sea, partitioning the 'big' and 'small' sections of beach, although they're technically one area.

A little bridge connects these two sections of beach, the famous dunes emerging in full view on the larger side. You can gaze across the expanse of beach leading on to the Valley of Diamonds, a monumental sand dune that is traditional for walking groups and families to climb throughout the seasons. To the right is both a small white castle at the top of the beach and a building that hosts seaweed baths, a tradition that dates back decades and which tourists still travel from afar to experience. And beyond the castle is Enniscrone's popular pier. It's among Ireland's most walker-friendly beaches and one of the most aesthetically pleasing to the eye. On any given day, the Atlantic might rage or bask, its waves crashing or lying quietly, the foam trickling in like a whisper on the breeze.

To make the most of the beach for recreational purposes with a pet dog, handlers ventured out with the retreating tide. Dogs were allowed to run freely off the lead before 9 a.m., so my plan was to use it every morning, allowing Oscar to embrace a landscape that jars, visually at least, with his physical appearance; it is a sight to see a long-haired sheepdog running on a beach. Oscar advanced with the bravado of a child learning to walk. He moved at a significant pace from sea to sand, galloping with his ears pinned back and his coat pushing against the breeze. On the first retreat from the dunes in the direction home, the herding activity I came to think of as magical in its form reappeared – that creeping and crouching behaviour. The beach became, for the first time that week, a stage on which to observe the beauty of animality.

One morning, we reached the estuary at the western end of the beach, the point at which most walkers change course. Oscar slowed to a halt. He pointed his nose out firmly in front and crept along on all fours in a crouching pose. He was fascinated by a dog a short distance away. I filmed him on my phone to capture the movement, such was the satisfaction in watching an animal's instinct displayed with clinical precision. It was not unlike witnessing the concentration of a young Roger Federer as he takes to Centre Court at Wimbledon. Any attempt to distract him from the white blob that had appeared in his eyeline was futile. At certain intervals, Oscar would cease his creeping motion, do 'a clapper' (as it's known in herding lingo, when the dog 'claps' its chest down to the ground instead of standing or moving) and stare obsessively at the incoming object, then move ever so slowly, like he was intentionally acting in slow motion. He was so taken in by this dog that appeared in the distance. His herding instinct had, of course, revealed itself before, but it truly blossomed on the wide open spaces of the beach that morning. A holidaying walker stopped to declare, 'You need to get that guy working.' 'Yeah, I must,' I awkwardly replied.

It became our holiday ritual. Walking to the estuary and back, as the Atlantic air seeped into our skin, had a mythical bent; a heroic push into the liminal space of sea and sand. On the vast beach each morning, the same handlers and dogs were out in force, taking in the fullness of the landscape. And, every morning, the same white speck appeared in the distance. The sight came to elicit the same instinctual moves in Oscar: crouch, creep, stare. He hunched, fully engrossed by the object in his midst until about a hundred yards from the evidently smaller dog. His tail wagged by way of a greeting, yet he never barked. Some mornings, the stalking would last for more than five minutes before excitement overcame him just as the other dog came within earshot of us. Some handlers were put off by the level of absorption displayed, but the ballerina-like elegance of movement delighted most who looked on. An animal so deeply absorbed in stalking the other was such an alluring sight. Unsurprisingly, one morning a curious farmer approached me, having seen Oscar perform.

'He's a classy worker,' he said. 'You can see he's got serious pedigree.' A lengthy conversation ensued, for an hour or more, as I told him the story of finding Oscar on a derelict farm in County Clare. I never got the name of the farmer, nor his phone number. But his talk of 'eye' (referencing Oscar's ability to control the herd using the famous 'collie stare') and 'bone' – his elegant movement – stayed with me. Oscar, he told me, displays the movement typical of pedigree. Again, the references to 'work' and 'pedigree' fuelled my curiosity about these dogs, bringing a sense of wonder that Oscar was displaying such a keen aptitude for a particular job. But however much pleasure his elegance on the wide-open beach had given me aesthetically, it also brought about significant unease; in being kept as a pet, perhaps Oscar was being deprived of doing what he was fated to do? Maybe companionship was only a minor recompense for losing his work on the farm. The beach display was a signal to get moving. Something had to be returned, a way had to be found for Oscar to 'flourish'. And yet it was no easy task. He would probably need a herd of sheep, for a start.

Returning home from holiday, I reviewed the video capturing his movements and his deep concentration, staring down the dog in his eyeline, breaking it to momentarily flick a look in my direction. More than a century of breeding had instilled in this particular breed a way of working that has fundamentally altered the prey drive. As a result of this intensive breeding, border collies were classified as a proper breed in the late nineteenth century, becoming the most popular herding dog across twentieth-century Britain and Ireland. While some histories suggest an Irish origin for the breed, another denotes an origin in Northumberland with the emergence of 'Old Hemp' at the end of the nineteenth century – a legendary sheepdog said to have sired more than 200 puppies. The more pictures of Old Hemp I scrutinised, the more my companion – who seemed to always look to me for guidance (and whose guidance to me seemed to be a kind of care) – registered as a 'person' in my mind. I was consumed

with returning something, to let him 'flourish' around what is otherwise known as work.

As my research into the origin of sheepdogs on the Scottish and English borderlands progressed, I became more attuned to the physical similarities between Oscar and Old Hemp. They were both of a similar height and both looked with an intense stare. One was a border collie from the Irish legacy, the other from the English–Scottish border, yet they were so alike. The border region of Northumberland, falling on the English side of the border with Scotland is not so different geographically to Ireland's midwest region, where I had found Oscar. On the Scottish side, the council areas of Dumfries & Galloway and the Scottish Borders run counter to Northumberland and Cumbria in England, with both sides subjected to dramatic weather. The rolling hills and marshes brought on by significant rainfall coexist with open terrain susceptible to high winds. Dogs are a necessary part of the workforce in such landscapes, used to keep track of and control over the flocks of sheep so plentiful in the region. So, when the word 'border collie' was spoken to me, a sheepdog appeared on a mountain top, on one side Scotland, the other England, nation-states that Benedict Anderson likes to call imagined communities. Borders, after all, may be marked by mountains and geographical features, but they may also be invisible.

It is often said by the Irish that inhabitants of the border counties between the Republic of Ireland and Northern Ireland can travel without any awareness of stepping from one nation into another. Perhaps grief demands a similar passage. We look for signposts to signal a transition from one area to another, but without this guidance, the space is vast and unknown. We ramble, without clear direction or understanding of where we are, trying to reach a mountain-top, a peak, like the collie in my mind's eye, but unable to catch even a clear sight of the destination, unable to cross over into the next land.

The in-between borderland made me ever more curious. Maybe, I thought, grieving pertains to a similar state of suspension between here and there, now and then. Perhaps I was in the middle and did not know. Sometimes I thought, *The bad is yet to come*, impervious to the fact that waiting was a form of grief. And sometimes I wondered whether shock is a waiting game, fuelled by the desire to feel when numbed from feeling itself. Maybe borders are passageways between emotional states, some of which have not yet been travelled – the liminal spaces the grieving can stumble through without direction.

When I took that film of Oscar running on Enniscrone beach, news was breaking about borders that might not be borders much longer. Northern Ireland, so long in a politically controversial union with Britain, had voted to remain a member of the European Union. Brexit, perhaps the stickiest political event of my lifetime, had reopened debates about borders between the North and Republic. On the beach that morning, as the Brexit debate raged in the media, my time with Oscar seemed to turn on a tradition common to both our islands, exceeding my understanding of division. It was a heritage so deep to Britain and Ireland. My dog's ancestors came from neither here nor there. They came from a space between. Handlers came from Scotland, from England, from the North and from the Republic. But the dogs came from the in-between: the borderlands of life.

4

From Another World

I met Tom in the woods when he was working for the local Tidy Town group – volunteers who were in the process of building feeders for the red squirrel population, a vital part of the forest ecosystem. It was early summer 2018, shortly after our Enniscrone holiday, and I was running the trail in a feverish state, with Oscar by my side, when two men appeared. I knew one of them – my neighbour, Gordon – but not the other. Aware that some people are terrified of dogs, I grasped at the lead immediately. But Oscar was his usual affable self and the second man, who introduced himself as Tom, began to rub Oscar's stomach and compliment his good looks. Because he spoke with such passion about dogs, it was obvious he was the Tom who was a breeder of sheepdogs and whom I had heard about. He had bred in the past, he explained, but not any more. He did, however, have several dogs at home.

Tom and I kept in contact and, soon after, I showed him the film of Oscar on the beach. He recommended bringing

Oscar to sheep, both at the end of lambing season and later in the summer, by which time the lambs would have matured. That summer, ad hoc lessons in working herds took place upon my casual encounters with Tom, during which I tapped into his wealth of practical knowledge. Tom had attended trials across Ireland and Britain throughout the decades and had even imported dogs from Wales. He had amassed an immense knowledge of farming traditions throughout Ireland's midwest.

Tom and I had a common interest in country life. Against my urban instincts as a teenager, I became accustomed to the country ways, but I was, of course, a townie. However, I understood the rural/urban divides. I could hold a conversation with farmers about silage or the lambing season or dairy farming. I was well informed about the stuff that preoccupied farmers and had developed a good grasp of what motivates those who live close to the land. For this reason, I forged an organic relationship with Tom.

During that time, the sale of my father's estate loomed large and the eventual loss not just of a home, but the traces left behind, hit harder than expected. It was a strange few months. The saying 'It's more than bricks and mortar' makes reference to the family loss of a house and home that's so often a springboard for remembrance. Until the sale, the journey to Cloondarone helped maintain the illusion that my father might step out from behind a shed at any moment, or come wandering around the corner. And in the grip of shock, those ghostly premonitions are a source of comfort, feeding the will to persist. Every time I got into the car to journey west, to drive along the motorway that connects Limerick to Galway, some part of me was still accustomed to going home to see my father alive. But as the time passed, and as grief's clutch embraced me, the estate began to look and feel a little more run-down. The plans to sell were firmly put in motion – first the land and then the house – making the illusion of my father's return lose its power over me. By the summer, the impending sale of the house and the land had copper-fastened and became a reality, bringing the weight of loss crashing down. Somehow, if the farm was in the family's name, the fantasy of my father's return would remain intact.

August soon rolled around and it was time. Tom was training a one-year-old short-haired collie, an energetic bitch considered to have a high ceiling – or much potential – called Nell. He agreed to give Oscar a run at the sheep with her. It was a chance to finally see if he'd had any training. While I strongly suspected that he had been trained, his previous life was still such an unknown and, when the day finally arrived to meet with Tom and Nell, a rush of excitement pulsated through me. Undertaking a herding activity, although far from replicating my father's passion for horses, was a process I felt he would have enjoyed if he were still alive. It lifted my spirits. A scene took shape in my imagination of a parallel life: when my father was staying with us, in the new house that he had never seen. We were drinking tea, waiting for Tom to call. The plan was to follow Tom to Rearcross, to the sheep. We set off along the back roads towards the farm, passing the little dip and then rise in the road that signalled the entrance to the Clare Glens and then on again. In my mind's eye, Dad was sitting in the passenger seat beside me, with Oscar lying in the back.

I was now making that drive. I was in the real world, yet navigating the speculative world of imagination, ushering my father back. A film played in the cinema of my mind as the car rolled along the winding road to Tom's place. The ghostly presence of a past tense filtered through the window, slowly joining the present. From Tuam to Limerick, from Enniscrone to Connemara, to the vistas of Tipperary, fiction met reality as the borderline between the world of facts and desires slowly melted with the sun.

Dad stared out the window at the Limerick–Tipperary border. He asked where we were going. 'Tipperary. I'm giving something back to Oscar.' Then I remember that Dad died in Tipperary, on his way home from that point-to-point in Ballingary. When his bedroom was being cleared, numerous out-of-date cheques from point-to-points he worked on were found. 'He never cashed them,' Loe McDonagh said. 'He was giving something back.'

Perhaps I was also trying to make good on a return, to pay back the favour to Oscar I believed he had paid me, to build back his core being. I told Dad that Oscar had shepherded me through the months of shock and pain. 'It sounds crazy, but he came into my life when you went away. I'm repaying the favour.' Dad looked at me sternly before a wry smile broke out across his face 'Okay,' he said, 'I didn't tell you that I was leaving.' He pushed his reading glasses up on to his crown and peered away abruptly – ashamed, perhaps – to look at me. I caught his gaze, but all I could see was an old man, unlike the version of him that's etched in my mind. I wanted to ask him if he sent Oscar to me. But he was gone, his seat empty. There was no outburst, no tears requiring me to pull the car over. There was only the sadness that traces of the dead leave in the base of our self, long after they depart. The window was pulled up as I turned to Oscar. 'I know you know,' I said, passing the hills marking the entrance to Tipperary.

I thought back on the long-distance journeys – my father driving, me in the passenger seat – to some event or other in another county or city. He would pull the car into a lay-by or a petrol station, roll his seat back and, within seconds, settle into a snore. Then, ten minutes or so later, he awoke and began shaking his face a little, rubbing his eyes before starting up the car. I remember driving through Wales in 1996 to begin a semester at the University of Exeter as he regaled me with old tales of Celtic myth, before diverting to Stonehenge to feel the might of it all around us.

I reminisced on the return from Limerick Races on 28 December 2013, with 10-year-old Anton in the back and the car being distinctly buzzy. My father was convinced by Faugheen's brilliance, his spirits heightened by the industry of such a wonderful horse. It was another one of those special days when the magic of the Irish countryside infected our spirits. That act of simply being in the car together was soon replicated, many years later, by a dog nestling in the back seat.

Tom's jeep crept along the road to Rearcross, manoeuvring bends and turns. We followed. The road began to rise at the Newport GAA grounds. Some kilometres after, we peered across at the definitive regional trait: the valleys. Driving through such populated landscapes, with their valleys, elongations and falls, the last bloom of summer had an expressive allure. There was excitement as the car rocked back and forth approaching an oasis of farmland. It was a point beyond which the beauty of the Limerick–Tipperary borderlands stood out in their expansive grandeur. We pulled in at a little slope on a byroad, a few kilometres before Rearcross village centre. I recognised the road at once as an old route I cycled many times without knowing that this small boreen that led from it existed. The Newport–to–Thurles road, past Rearcross, is one of the region's better roads and one of the reasons it makes for such good cycling. It is well marked with practically no potholes. For this reason, following Tom felt something like a transition, a bridge into old Ireland. It was like a mysterious netherworld in counterpart to the real, a boreen with a small mullet of grass running up its middle pathway, marking the point when things turn to very rural, where modern Ireland meets its past.

I parked, got out and put the lead around Oscar's neck to stop him from wandering down to the main road. Once he was secure, we began to make our way to the field where Tom was waiting. He had a rope tied to the clippings on Nell's collar to allow her to circle the pen and build up her familiarity with a flock of sheep. Inside the field as the gate shut behind us, the painterly appearance of hemmed-in bushes stood out to me like a flash of light, a field gorgeously decorated by purple touches of rhododendron. The place had a dream-like quality, a serenity in a kind of hidden romantic idyll. The pen in the centre of the field held seven ewes. They were exceptionally large – bigger than I had imagined them to be – dwarfing Nell, a slim smooth-haired collie. Tom travelled here two or three times a week to train Nell. He took his time moving her back and forth in a near trance-like execution, enticing her to herd when the pen opened. He then decided – shouting back to me about his decision – to open the pen in order to test the efficacy of Nell's training. As soon as the pen opened, the sheep ran out in a small but coherent grouping. Nell ran after the sheep at near full speed, chomping at the bit – and at the tails of the frightened ewes.

'Stop! Stop!' I heard Tom shout, tripping over his wellingtons as he broke into a run. He raced through the field, with stick in hand, frantically trying to stop Nell nipping aggressively at the sheep, and only slowed once it was clear that she had simply been taken aback by the suddenness of the sheep leaving the pen in droves. Oscar looked upon the scene, oblivious to the unfolding chaos. It was like some comical reworking of the scene in *Withnail and I* when a lone bull confronts the protagonists as they travel home from the village with groceries. In the film, the principal characters, the struggling actors 'Withnail' and his compatriot known only as 'I', decamp from London to rural Wales, from the urban metropolis to its opposite. In this scene, the pair walk through a field where the stone walls are like great wedges set between green expanses. In a spirit of bonhomie, they wave at the farmer whom they have previously been in contact with. Stepping down from his tractor, the farmer shouts to warn them of a bull that's not yet apparent to the pair. In one of the great comic moments of modern British cinema, the bull intuits that the gate is open and manages to make its way into the field. Withnail gives the bag of groceries to 'I' before jumping the wall, leaving 'I' to face the bull alone. At this point, the farmer is on his way down to the field and starts to administer advice to the scared 'I'.

Eventually, not wholly unlike the way the bull scene drama concludes in *Withnail and I*, Tom caught Nell and was able to put the rope back around her neck. He got the sheep in line and moved them into a corner, all the while holding Nell. I walked over to where he was stood and tried to coax Oscar into something that resembled a herding motion – before realising he wasn't bothered by it.

'He probably needs to go around the pen on the rope to give him an extra push,' Tom said, 'although he might be too accustomed to the domestic.'

Oscar lay on his stomach with his tongue out, staring at the scene.

'Look, we'll come back again,' I replied. 'He doesn't seem that concerned and the ewes are so big.'

Standing on the grass that day, as the ewes towered over Oscar, the difference in scale appeared to intimidate him, as if they weren't actually sheep at all but some variant of cattle – the animals I had come to understand he was terrified of. Lambs? Fine. Large ewes? No thanks. The beauty of the setting – the purple of the rhododendron cast against the lush green of Ireland – impressed upon me more than any acute transformation in Oscar from a pet to a working dog. I tried. We had both tried to see if Oscar could pursue, unfettered, a herding life. But it wasn't to be – or he wasn't that bothered.

His herding instincts were confined to small poodle-like dogs on the beach, lamb-like in their stature. His herding behaviour was fundamentally different to that of Nell; she ran whippet-like around the field in the prescribed circular manner, her head turned inwards at the flock, while Oscar crouched while bending down, using his eye to control the animal in his stead.

Soon, he jumped up and down, before lying submissively on his tummy. Maybe, as the cliché went, a dog's personality mirrored that of its master. I was neither farmer nor shepherd. It wasn't the functionality of sheep herding that had attracted me – getting the sheep in line – but the aesthetic: the beauty of a dog running in counterpoint to its handler. Maybe Oscar was destined for work of a different kind. Maybe he was like me – 'of the country but not a part of it'. I watched him in the field, contemplating the times I had stood in an arena adjacent to my father's house as a teenager, observing Dad working the horses for which I had no natural affinity. He wanted so much to instil the desire in me to be something I knew I would never be. Maybe Oscar and I had bonded because we both lacked something: he was not a cattle dog or a sheepdog, and I was not a farmer or a shepherd in any real conventional sense. We had come together by chance.

As I looked upon Oscar that day, something important about the coileán made itself known to me. Maybe it was to do with suffering and what it means to watch another suffer. A certain type of person always comes to the rescue to fix, that desire to rescue predicated on the fear of suffering. The fixer is unable to watch another suffer as they cannot bear to feel another's pain. I realised, when looking back, that my grasp

of 'flourishing' was based on a desire to rescue and fix. More than anything, I wanted to give something back to Oscar that I had come to believe he had lost: I wanted to fix his core being. Maybe I thought by fixing him I could also fix myself, as if I was mopping up the puddle, returning something I myself had lost. Or maybe the attempt to fix another person was a deflection from the pain nestled in me, repressed into my bones. All the focus on a dog, projecting my deepest dreams and fantasies, was a dereliction of duty towards the self. It was only when gazing at Tom, Oscar and the ewes, that I experienced an epiphany: our companionship was not about fixing a human or a nonhuman. It was about a rescuing journey that involves another journeying with me, and me journeying with another – in symbiosis. This is what dissolving into a puddle of rain means. This is the essence of love and companionship.

Oscar moved up and down, before turning his gaze away. I walked over to the edge of the field to hug him. It wasn't to be. I thanked Tom for his patience and went back to the car with Oscar.

Companionship, John the groomer had told me, was an art of being together. I saw it. Being with me was a form of 'work' for Oscar – like running after sheep in a field. To be my companion, to foster a relationship with another organism, was the work a maker had designed for him. I began to take great pleasure in this discovery on the drive home through Tipperary that afternoon, thinking about a comment made to me on the border collie forum. It was a response to my query as to why Oscar ate his food when we were all going to bed. I was informed that border collies will often wait until everyone was curled up, the house was quiet and sleep beck-oned. The house rests and they then feel comfortable enough to eat. 'Work' is done and the herd sleeps. Sheepdogs are really helpers, as scientists would say, in symbiosis. They are lichens of the animal world. They settle when a family settles. I fell upon this realisation on peering into the field, like a mirror reflecting my image to me.

Back at home, the bowl was left beside the basket on the floor. Oscar stared up with gentle eyes. He lay against the wall, his front paw lifted in my direction. No matter how much was there, he waited for the person feeding him to leave the room for his work for the day to be done. And then, like magic, an empty bowl waited for collection the next day. Each time was the same, like clockwork.

About a week after our trip to Rearcross to see Tom, I lay on the garden lawn playing with Oscar. I watched him wig-gling on his back, his thick coat bristling in the summer sun. He was groaning and grunting but still not barking. That he did not bark was distressing to me and I had even considered asking the vet to see if he had been operated on to stop him from barking – as was done to some dogs. Maybe the constant barking had been too much for a previous owner to cope with. Or maybe he was too submissive to let out a bark? Or had he been trained not to? The truth is I had no idea why he did not bark – and it was starting to bother me more and more.

Oscar's silence was part of our lives. To some extent, it was a blessing. There was no persistent drone carried through the night, no short sharp shocks when a cat sauntered across the lawn. His silence was a marker of the weeks and months he had spent alone. That day, in breaks between playing with Oscar, while stretched out on the lawn together, I was making my way through a book about trauma that included a chapter focused on Holocaust survivors who became parents. I thought about these survivors, as the text informs, who did not speak about their experiences in the camps. They stayed silent even with their children – a wound passed between generations in silence. Children of survivors could, however, sense the pain, the trauma that was never actually spoken of. The Belgian filmmaker Chantal Akerman was a child of one such survivor. The impact of her mother's lifelong silence was explored by Akerman throughout her film work, like a scar that travelled through the corridors of time. It was not until her mother Natalia (Nelly) approached her death in her late eighties that the silence about the past broke through a little, a revelation wonderfully detailed in Akerman's memoir *My Mother Laughs*. Even those familiar with the trajectory of Chantal's career found her matter-of-fact relay of the moment her mother spoke strangely alluring. One day, Natalia talked of dying in 'that place' – the concentration camp. There was no real drama as such. The silence between mother and daughter broke down, but the event causing it in the first place could not be whisked away.

Perhaps part of the trauma that persisted for survivors like Natalia came from realising that talking itself could not 'cure'. There was no face-off between good and evil, no point at

which good prevails. There was just the acceptance of the past. There was no finality, just movement back and forth, just words to mark the event. Of course, I did not find an equivalence between Natalia's decades-long silence after surviving the Holocaust and my concerns about a dog not barking. But Oscar's silence was affecting me more and more. It led me back, increasingly, to the time before I knew him, to what might or might not have been. Oscar was more and more a 'person' in my eyes with each passing year and I began to conceive of his unwillingness to bark as a sign of deep trauma. Oscar did not bark, I speculated, because those whom he loved abandoned him. He was abused by fellow beings.

My thoughts brought me back to a blustery morning in my early twenties when an unruly sight on Enniscrone beach confronted me like a phantom in the night. It was a typically rainy day sometime in the summer of 1993 and bucketloads of seaweed had been washed up upon the shore from the previous night's tide. Balls of suds had stuck to the sand and retreating waves motioned in a tidal lurch from dawn until lunch. In the distance, over by the estuary, where the River Moy meets the Atlantic Ocean, people were huddled together in small groups, standing over what seemed, from a distance, to be a collection of washed-up objects of considerable size. In the drizzle, I struggled to make out the objects in question and quickened my pace to quell my rising curiosity. I had never seen so many people on the beach on a wet day. What were they doing? What were the objects? I approached the first cluster of people and forced my way through the outer ring to see what they were looking at.

On the beach was a dead dolphin. Grains of sand stuck to the creature's skin, yet the dolphin looked infused with life. Its skin had not rotted to any degree and the people standing over it kept the scavenging seagulls overhead at bay. Motionless, the creature proffered an angelic half smile, shimmering in the light. I stared at it for upwards of five minutes, consumed by its beauty. At the next group, I was met by another deathly sight. Twelve dolphins in total had been washed up on the shore with the tide. The corpses were out of context – mammals but fish out of water.

That afternoon in the pub, it was suggested that the school of dolphins was not in fact washed up. A stranger suggested to me that a dolphin had contracted syphilis and rather than allow the disease to spread throughout the school and kill each dolphin one by one – to take the school out in degrees – the dolphins acted accordingly to stem the disease. Years later, thinking of the story and looking into the issue, it was unclear whether dolphins could carry sexually transmitted diseases in seawater, but at the time the story had an authenticity about it. The dolphins, so the theory went, allowed the tide to draw them in, in an act of collective suicide. They had witnessed the deterioration of their fellow beings and, sensing their own imminent demise, had acted for the betterment of the group. And so, to quell the spread of disease to each member, the affected individuals swam through the Atlantic Ocean to their eventual death – all for one and one for all, a cliché destined to capture the mindset of such special mammals.

As the encounter with dead dolphins returned to memory, that blustery morning on the beach prompted me to recall

Oscar's silence. I was fascinated by the idea of animals intuiting something wrong and acting accordingly: a response to disease, albeit one that can elicit pain and death. Dolphins, like sheepdogs, are very intelligent animals, known to forge lasting relationships with humans. Think of Fungie, Ireland's famous dolphin who performed for his keep for decades on Ireland's Dingle peninsula.

My memory of the beached dolphins came from dwelling on sensitive nonhuman animals who were responsive to the same life travails as human beings. My submissive sheepdog did not bark and I wanted to know why. Like the dolphins, maybe he too had suffered from severe loss. Maybe his silence derived from his fear of cattle or his sensitivity to my tonal variation or was a legacy of abuse bestowed upon him as a pup. Maybe Oscar had drifted through the village of Kilkishen – a glorious near-spiritual animal, peripatetic in search of company, wandering into the light – only to be kicked back to abusive shouts, such as 'Scram, you dirty sheepdog!' or 'Go on, get out of here!', hurled in anger. Then my sheepdog, no less capable of love than you or me, returned to the farm. The time before – the mystery of his past – manifested as an aura of improbability, of what could have been, as I contemplated the silence between us. I imagined Oscar running along the driveway, throngs of cattle rushing to the fence in response to him. I pictured him spurting up towards a cow from the rear, pushing the herd back into the field one by one. And then a kick in his direction. Spit with traces of blood flowed out from his mouth. His head was rattled hard so that whiplash manifested itself for a few hours. Every time he approached cattle from that point on, he was immobilised, fear coursing through his body. He afterwards took a vow of silence until, one summer afternoon, messing about with his new master on the lawn, it arose from out of the abyss.

Oscar barked.

It was a sticky, humid August day. Buttercups and daisies were radiant on our lawn, birdsong rang out and cattle were sighing in adjacent fields. I tumbled on the grass, trying, as best I could, to initiate enough joyfulness to trigger the 'zoomies', the frenetic activity experienced by dogs in moments of excitement. A 'Frenetic Random Activity Period' is when a dog runs recklessly at pace, consumed by a feeling so intense it's nearly impossible to stay still. Clapping was supposed to trigger this in breeds such as Oscar's, making him more conducive to play. I was lying on the lawn, Oscar hovering above me, and I was clapping to my heart's content. Then it came, unexpectedly. A sound, a bark, a monotone declaration pushed out into the wind like a cry from a siren. Oscar pointed his nose, his face set in a sideways direction, his mouth allowing wolf-like teeth to protrude outwards, like a glacial formation set on an Antarctic coastline. Then he barked repeatedly, again and again. Before I had witnessed the declaration in full, Ylva and Karl ran from the garage to ask me, 'Is that Oscar?' Standing up to explain the events, I clapped again. Oscar then reacted to the stimulus as requested. He cocked his nose in the air and barked loudly. I ran over to hug him. Like a child who had been afraid to speak, Oscar had finally found his voice. The silence between us evaporated.

Perhaps life's high points are totally subjective. What means everything to some means little to others. Life turns in a blink. Imagine having to convince a friend who has little to no interest in interspecies relations that a dog barking, the bane of so many urban dwellers, had become an infinite source of joy. A dog barked and everything changed, unpacking the deepest seats of emotion. Grey clouds were gathering that afternoon, closing in on the sun. Bumblebees were making their way across the garden, stopping here and there, before slowly moving on. Blackbirds were whistling in song. Then a dog began to bark. He barked so loud a silent night seemed to give way to a word-filled day.

Natalia eventually spoke about the camps to Chantal as her death approached, but she had little time to explore the ramifications of the immense issue at stake. Her daughter waited all her life to hear her mother speak ('I realised that my heart had died'), to put words on the pain bequeathed to her in the silent, sometimes corporeal aporia of memory. When she finally opened up, her words had a muted effect. Language could not fill the void between generations. Language could not measure up to the horror. Natalia spoke about her symbolic death at Auschwitz, but it was words and more words. By then, words as symbols were not enough.

In contrast to Natalia, for whom speaking did little to assuage a lifetime in the shadow of the event ('apart from the best bits she couldn't say anything'), Oscar's bark was a transformative event in our life. It pushed out like a message from above, but it was never fully apparent what had been the trigger. Care? Companionship? A symbiotic relationship between organisms that harvested vital nutrients for both? Maybe it was that thing that turns two into one: love. I thought back to that day on the lawn, basking in the joy that came from a sudden burst of sound, thinking of the evening Oscar had first come home with us, the image of a dishevelled animal burning in memory. Two years later, everything had changed. The dog I had feared might attack when confined in the car had turned out to be the most sensitive being I could imagine. It was a rescue act in one sense but, as the months turned into years, and as a bark rang out from the place of love, it became evidently clear to me that the rescue act ran in more than one direction. The bark was greater than a break in the silence between us. It was an acknowledgment of the loss carried within ourselves. For Oscar, it was the loss of his original safe space, the place where he was reared as a pup. For me, it was the loss of my father. The bark was a mirror held up to a soul that seemed to resonate between us, a beating drum that sounded out the silence I associated with shared trauma.

My father passed away on a Sunday. I received news from my uncle and had to identify the body at the hospital, after which I drove home immediately to help with arrangements. So much had to be done, one of which was to rehome a pup my father had adopted before his death. (I was tempted that day to keep the wee one, but it was complicated as we were in a rental property.) The other task, of course, was the funeral. Oscar's first loud utterance, for some reason, returned my thoughts to that week in June 2016, which had also been sweltering hot. Awash with involuntary sensations on the morning of the funeral – the smell of heavily pollinated air, the sound of tractors in the distance, the slow hum of grazing cattle – my eulogy referenced neighbours and friends dropping in to see my father for coffee. Sunlight poured in through windows, horses moved freely in adjacent fields, butterflies pressed against the clear exposure of glass. Memory, I wrote that same morning, transformed instantly – as sudden death descended on me – into singular jewels of a now-precious time. I came to understand, looking back, the things I was comfortable writing about – all the memories of my father's life – and those that I would have to stay silent on: the utter cruelty of the accident. I found it too difficult to reflect on the event that led to my father's death and it was only years later that I visited the scene of the accident. I didn't leave flowers there or build a monument. Instead, Ylva drove the car home. When we got back, I was exhausted, like a weight had been placed on me; each time I referenced the event, the weight on me increased proportionally.

But then Oscar barked in August 2018. And I too began to speak about the accident, to visit the site and accept the fatigue that driving to it entailed. Change came. Then, one morning, not long after 'the bark', I passed by Oscar's black-and-white profile at the patio-room door, distorted through a new glass panel. He was waiting to go to the woods as usual. Then I heard a bark – once, maybe twice – summoning me. Soon after, it became commonplace for Oscar to wander into the house and bark at me at will. He wagged his tail and baited me to hurry. In due course, I cherished these moments of interruption. I loved his eccentric turn to the wind and his bellowing holler, as if to say, 'C'mon, my friend, you need to get moving.'

In time, the bark was a demand to accompany me everywhere. He would travel to collect the kids from events, go with me to the supermarket, help with the daily chores. Stoically perched in the back seat, he stuck his nose out the window to suck in the air, all accompanied by his now-trademark bark. The bark was less of an interaction, as he always communicated his joy physically, like a jubilant child playing in a yard. It was more about his confidence. The silence had been a way of diminishing his presence, reducing himself around us. Similarly, in the periods of intense grieving, I lacked the confidence in myself, often wondering why others would seek my company, why they would want to be around me. I felt purposeless, like I had nothing to offer the world. Maybe the fact that I never returned my father's call when driving home from Ballybunion that day affected me more than I knew; deep down I blamed myself for not responding to it like a dutiful son. And maybe Oscar also lost all confidence in himself. He was submissive, too eager to please, needy and devoid of something. The bark was a fight in him, and the battle in me, like pushing up from under a wave to draw breath.

On a brisk evening during that same summer of 2018, I called out Oscar's name from the perch of the back door and heard a rattling noise from the fence beside the trees. I called his name again. More rustling. A hole had opened up in the fence, making a little channel between our property and the next. Our nonagenarian neighbour Michael was a retired creamery manager whom I was told suffered from Parkinson's disease. Frail and thin, he was nonetheless mentally sharp. I took comfort in talking with him, discussing traditions that had ceased in the information age. Ireland was a poor and mainly agricultural country in his youth. Emigration was the natural order as gainful employment was thin on the ground. Michael spoke of a time before television or the internet, a time when newly installed phones transformed the island. I listened attentively, having moved from the city to the countryside to be close to the kind of rural wisdom that he seemed to possess in spades. He looked like an ageing Woody Allen and his often cantankerous responses to my many observations channelled the grey area between the endearing and the mad.

It concerned me to think Oscar was venturing off into Michael's property. It was an additional concern that he was wandering over and back at will. When he was out of sight, I felt uneasy about his whereabouts. One day, Michael met me on the road and I mentioned the gap between the houses. He replied that a friend would soon fix it – he was adamant that it was his responsibility. Weeks then passed and Oscar still moved in and out between the properties. The hole was still there. Some evenings, I walked over to Michael's house calling out Oscar's name, only to discover him stretched out on the grass like a nude from a lost Manet. The sight was strangely discomforting. It was difficult to square Michael's renowned fastidiousness (he always did what he said) with the gap in the fence between us. Michael, known as a pernickety creamery manager in his day, was proud and stubborn. Yet the hole was left exposed and Oscar seemed to be spending more and more time going through it. My interest in what was luring him increased. Was the garden full of rabbits? Was he drifting even further afield? What exactly was he at?

A few weeks later, the issue was still unresolved. Oscar's name was called out again, yet he was nowhere to be found. I peeked over the fence to catch him off guard, trying to discover why he was so quick to make his way over beyond. But he wasn't there. A frightened rabbit stared at me from the lawn, but there was no evidence of Oscar. My next step was to investigate the hole in the fence as a possible corridor. Maybe it led from Michael's into the field of a property that sits further on the outskirts of the village – a big green field that recedes into ditches and trees. The landscape there came to life in the evening as silhouettes pushed against the reddening skies, trees stretching up on high. But drifting out to the field, I still couldn't find him. When I whistled over and over from the backyard, he took an age to return to me. When he did finally emerge, he was hunkered down to suggest he was acting in subordination. He was like a child caught with his hand in the cookie jar.

I lost count of the evenings spent peeking into the garden of the home originally built for Michael's daughter (Michael would relocate to it when the home he had been living in was purchased by us). Oscar was rarely there. Hunched over, Michael seldom ventured out. I peered in to check he hadn't fallen or been hurt in some way. But no matter how much time was spent looking in, often upwards of five minutes, there was no sign of Oscar. I suspected he was in there, but I couldn't be sure. Returning at random times in the day to call his name, the rustling would start before he reappeared, bent in submission, guilty as charged. And on it went. The gap in the fence between the houses remained.

Weeks went by before I considered asking Michael again whether it was best to stop Oscar straying. I thought at length about having Oscar neutered, taking the vet's advice to have him fixed if he began to roam. I even thought about altering the boundaries to include Michael's property, using an electrical collar device that shocks the dog if it breaks bounds. But some research soon put a stop to that idea.

One typical afternoon, when I was collecting the post, two small feet made their way into my field of vision. Michael was standing in front of me. He was bent down with a walking stick in his hand. His profile came into view as I realised he was carrying a small piece of paper.

'Michael,' I said. His head perked up and a frail, aged man peered up at me from behind thick-rimmed glasses. He was struggling to recognise me as his neighbour. A sharpness of mind was succumbing to the waves of time. 'It's Dara, Michael,' I said, venturing closer, my hands outstretched, trying to not scare him in any way. His wrinkly hands were thin and frail, veins popping like sinews. The pallor of his skin was noticeable against the grey pebbles littered along the road.

The conversation struggled to get going. Michael's doddery disposition, much increased even since we had moved in as neighbours, was more apparent to me. Age had finally caught up with him. Then a car raced by and birds flew up in the sky. Confusion relented into a buoyant smile. He lifted his

cane affirmatively. I turned around to see if there was anyone coming by to say hello, but it was just Oscar standing alone by the garage. His tail moved in sync with a body shuffle.

'There he is,' Michael said, his cane pointing at Oscar on arrival. Oscar made his way down a driveway covered with bristling pine needles and leaves, before sidling up beside Michael as though I wasn't there. A tinge of envy came over me; my dog's affection for me seemingly usurped. 'There he is,' Michael said again, his cane hitting the earth while he hunkered down to rub Oscar. A bond between the two that I had not known of made itself public. I was superfluous to the affection between them, a gooseberry in their midst. And then the full-blown epiphany arrived. My neighbour and my dog were not in fact strangers. They were, to all extents and purposes, friends.

'Look at that,' Michael said, pointing at Oscar. 'He loves the cocktail sausages and mash.' We laughed like before. Then rain began to trickle. Oscar pushed up against Michael with an intimacy purporting to an obvious truth of 'friendship'. I didn't need to speak. I was no longer curious as to his whereabouts and his wandering was no longer a concern. Of course, things needed to be fleshed out. Had Oscar made it into Michael's house? Or was he waiting at the back door? Was Michael cooking dinner for Oscar in his spare time? Or was he feeding him leftovers from his own dinner? Cocktail sausages and mash is children's food. A cocktail sausage was usually served at birthdays and associated events – food small enough to be consumed at ease. It was endearing as a matter of course to think that Michael was cooking for Oscar every evening, serving up dinner to his neighbour. But it also implied he had – to some extent – found a new friend during his final days on Earth.

My evening ventures to find Oscar no longer required an explanation. Those two being in cahoots was more than a tonic for joy. Every time I recalled the cane rising in front of Michael, sequestering Oscar into his orbit, I imagined two beings 'hanging out' in the backyard of Michael's small bungalow in a curious alteration of a human–animal relationship taking shape in the winter of a nonagenarian's life. Michael passed a week later. I was told he fell in his house and didn't have the wherewithal to get up. After being found, he passed some time after.

Good-hearted laughter, however, was a choice response to the cross-species friendship that flourished before his tragic passing. And from this, the unexpected took shape: the ghost of my father listened as I spoke about Michael and Oscar. The scene was set. We were in the kitchen in Murroe, discussing the discovery that day.

'Dad,' I said, 'a gap in the fence has the dog meandering through.'

'So what?' my father waspishly replied.

'The guy next door keeps feeding him his dinner,' I stressed.

A vigorous man walked over from the kitchen to the dining area, brushing off dust from his jacket. His hand was held in the air and he proffered a wink, before whispering, 'Won't it save you from feeding him?' before belting out a boorish hoorah. 'Do you think he'll stop roving now?' I remonstrated back to him. 'Maybe,' my father returned to me again, 'but aren't they having the craic together?' The ghost of a conversation ended with father and son heartily laughing into the wind.

After Michael's death, Oscar no longer ventured off into his property. Instead, he wandered off in other directions, mostly to the fenced astroturf pitch at the back of our garden. Murroe Park is a six-acre park area in the village, with a football and hurling pitch and a skate park. Much of the construction occurred during the years Oscar first arrived, intensifying through 2019 and on to today. A half-kilometre loop on the side of the pitch was spotlit throughout the winter months, a small component of a much bigger sports complex lying beside our house. During the construction, trees were removed from our garden. In the early days of Covid-19 that began more than a year after Michael died, a travel limit of two kilometres was imposed on citizens across the country. The park became immeasurably busier; people and dogs loitered there from dawn to dusk. I called out Oscar's name repeatedly one evening, only to eventually find him perched on his hind legs beside the pitch fence. He had managed to find a way out to it after the removal of the trees and was staring through the fence at some other dogs. He was deep in concentration and my call received no reaction. I walked over to him, put a lead around his neck and walked home. For some reason, the return walk provoked immense sadness in me. I had reason to be sad. My friend was not responding to my call. Recall – for some handlers the most important thing in an interspecies relationship – had dissipated in that moment.

Disappointment set in. My friend had more pressing interests: his own.

'Maybe it's the roaming the vet warned about,' I said to Ylva. The first sign of a dreaded wander? An extension of the visits to Michael's house? Maybe he needs a new friend? With all the pandemic restrictions in place, it was difficult to access basic services. For a time, it was difficult to even see a vet. Considerable time was taken up peering out the window every few minutes to see if Oscar was there. Each time I looked – I was working from home during those early days of the pandemic – a statue-like creature was at the fence. The grass was thick; the first draw of silage beckoned. New flowers fluttered on shoots of green and spring lurched into summer as starling chicks rattled in ducts. The travel restrictions transformed life; dogs were seen running the astropitch loop, ever-present on a landscape altered in one swoop. The first months of Covid restrictions precipitated new eyes; a new way of seeing the landscape.

Glenstal Abbey lay within the two-kilometre travel limits imposed by lockdown, but the forest and pitch remained the most accessible walks. In fact, we had not attempted the Glenstal route in any shape or form since that early aborted attempt. A scenic path sat on our doorstep, unused. But Covid was long and monotonous; one day lurched into the next and the world began to turn in upon itself. Everything close at hand suddenly became a prop in a new-found reality. Walking a dog brought an escape from the banal stay-at-home policy. And the Glenstal estate offered a new environment to explore in intimate detail.

For a while, we made the most of the six-kilometre cycle route that Glenstal offered. Oscar, at this point, stayed at home. Our walks together were mainly in the back field. It was difficult enough to remain the requisite distance from the other walkers and dogs that passed us along the monastery drive, and there was a constant need to suppress our socialising instincts. At a time when the pandemic was surging across Europe, there was also unprecedented good weather. The days passed in a surreal haze. On some days, the temperatures reached mid-summer levels and we cycled the route in only T-shirts and shorts. Passers-by smiled over in our direction, giving a jolt of village camaraderie at a time of our familial insulation. These little signals were careful reminders of a life lived before in its normality, a life we had taken for granted in our pre-Covid existence and that might or might not one day return. Maybe in a distant future?

New rituals took shape during lockdown – activities designed to keep our boredom at bay – while older ones proved difficult to maintain. Occasionally we ventured over to the Slieve Felim Way. We grabbed a Coke at the shop and turned off at the monument for a few kilometres before reaching the destination: the start of our great pilgrimage. The path traversing the mountain range between Murroe in County Limerick and the Silvermines in County Tipperary was an escape from all things Covid-related.

The lockdown went on and on, and the lack of a proper horizon to give life its spontaneous oomph began to impact everyone even more. There was no real goal; no sense of what lay beyond. Life was just a slow drift into the future with nothing to strive for. The Clare Glens were sealed off, the Slieve Felim lost all its allure and the woods we spent our mornings in became something of a prison into which the restrictions pushed us. It left us with very few choices.

I was hesitant about revisiting Glenstal with Oscar, yet he refused to walk Slieve Felim and kept roaming to the sports pitch to stare through the green fence. Seeing him there, tail wagging, entranced by another dog, saddened me. As happy as he seemed in my company, I felt his isolation acutely. Maybe our enforced solitude undergirded a burgeoning curiosity to interact with other dogs. Maybe the picture of Oscar staring – too shy to interact – had purpose and meaning. Had he been far too young when released from a litter as a puppy? Perhaps he craved company but did not 'understand' the dynamics of playful behaviour. No matter how much I chased after him or cajoled him to respond to my antics, he never seemed taken by a desire to chase a ball or Frisbee. He simply had no interest in pursuing it. I tried to coax him into chasing things with treats, but it just wasn't his thing.

Oscar craved being in the company of other beings, whether human or nonhuman. His intelligence, now that I am more confident in adjudging its meaning, is emotional: he has a remarkable ability to temper the mood. When a strong bond forms, the world of a collie can often seem consumed with the one job given to them. In most cases, these jobs are physical activities, such as herding or mountain rescue. But sometimes, I concluded, they transcend the physical into the metaphysical – and even the existential. Once, I asked a friend of mine why Oscar roamed to the pitch. He replied, 'He's curious about people. He's not used to people going out with their dogs and moving past the house at will. His world has changed utterly.' Like me, he needs the presence of others to get him through the day.

Yes, the world had changed and I decided that something more than the humdrum plod through the forest was needed. Walking the same route multiple times a day was grating on the soul. A shrunken world was a novelty at first, but it soon generated a dulling of the senses. Repetition made each day a monotonous simulation of the one before. Only so many off-the-cuff decisions can be taken away before a numbness akin to grief takes over. The days were made up of 'time' and it went by second by second. But there was something about anniversaries and birthdays – cyclical time – each year returning to the same date a little different. Something in my bones rattled and then I looked at the calendar. There it was, looming: 5 June.

The anniversary of my father's death, as usual, made its presence felt like a symbolic needle that returned all the adrenaline of the original event. A heaviness, physical in its fullness, consumed me once again. Oscar seemed fully aware that it was an important day for me and I was on my own – without either of my immediate family, my two sisters and mother. I so badly needed to do something to break out of the inertia.

'C'mon, let's go,' I said, clipping Oscar's lead onto his collar. 'Let's do Glenstal.' For some reason, I wanted to do the route again with him. Fortuitously – perhaps the anniversary itself, perhaps a desire to break the cycle – the time felt right.

We made it up the driveway in no time, the sun shining upon the abbey. The difference was not lost on me: now, we were companions – or soulmates, as some call it. Unlike that first time trying to do the loop, when I had to drag Oscar along the driveway and he resembled a sack of spuds, I was now happy to stride along with him, so at ease in each other's presence. We made it to the top and passed around the corner, where two miniature donkeys stood grazing, unperturbed by the many passers-by. A trail led down to tennis courts on one side, and another to a man-made lake. Gaining confidence that Oscar would not hit against the fence when quickening to a run, I began to slowly increase my speed. I had not intended to go for a run, but suddenly I was trotting with Oscar by my side. We wove our way, avoiding 'traffic' on the track. In the distance, a vehicle resembling a golf buggy appeared. I squinted to see the Glenstal insignia on the front of the vehicle. Someone was patrolling the grounds, enforcing Covid restrictions – or so it seemed. I thought about directing Oscar past the vehicle but, when I looked up, he was nowhere to be seen. As I got nearer, the buggy slowed down and a man stepped out. It was one of the Benedictine monks from the abbey, wearing a garment with a hanging hood, a cushion for his balding crown. His shoe tips peered out from beneath his habit.

Behind him, cattle moved sluggishly, grazing on only one side of the road. Black, white and brown clashed with a hue of green. It was like a pre-Raphaelite landscape bursting into life. Lebanese cedar were staggered side by side, flanking a track that opened onto pastures of grazing land. Where had

Oscar gone? I stepped closer to speak to the monk. He was whispering to himself. He seemed to be counting, but I struggled to discern the words from a short distance away. My gaze drifted with his along the hedges that marked the back end of the estate. Just below the skyline, I thought there was something moving, crawling at the rear of the herd. Thrown into a vivid daydream, I imagined it to be Oscar, the sheepdog, crouched behind a battalion of doddery cattle. He was stalking the group in the patchy grass, his stare fixed on the straggling one lurking at the back. Absorbed by the vision of a sheepdog in working mode, I reflected on the scene for what seemed a considerable time. My hand automatically moved upward to offer approval, but before I could complete the action, I was jolted back to reality when the monk seemed to turn in my direction. I found it difficult to speak. I had no idea what to say.

The herd were assembled at the gate, a tight-knit audience at the only entrance to the field. The different coloured cattle fused into an abstraction of form echoing Oscar's black-and-white hues. That so many cattle were gathered made me uneasy. Would the monk report Oscar for being off the lead? Was there poison along the fence? Was Oscar out there, beyond the gate? I began to drift off again. In the vision, Oscar popped his head up from behind the herd, staring with intent. He was concentrating on the job at hand, just as he had on Enniscrone beach. The monk was a farmer and Oscar was born of the wind, moving effortlessly in the ancient fields of Ireland.

As I passed the monk, thinking of saying hello, I kept my

head down in silence. I was caught in the thick of imaging: the monk farming the land, Oscar crouching on all fours in the adjacent field. In my daydream, Oscar worked the cattle into a group as the monk turned to ask, 'Where did you get him? How old is he?'

Then Oscar hurtled over, wagging his tail, his tongue set loose. As we ran together on that lush summer day, reverie and reality began syncing poetically as one, the old world beckoning. In front, the Glenstal pastures appeared startlingly green, summer rushing through with strength. Sunshine was forcing its way through grey-tinged clouds. Suddenly, life began to turn on its axis.

'I found him on a farm near Kilkishen,' I heard myself say, as the words themselves came to consciousness like a poem.

'But he comes from another world.'

As I approached the monk at Glenstal that day, my mind's imagery took the form of a film, Oscar its subject. I was the shepherd and Oscar was a cattle dog who had found his essence. I thought of the trusting relationship between a film director and subject needed to concoct scenarios that a director believes true to the character of the subject. But while I speculated about Oscar, I could not discuss his ambition with him. The dream was not a temporality to give much credence to in the canine mind. Dogs lived in the present, existing in the hum of life. In grief, humans avoided the present. There were too many daily markers of loss. Objects were symbolic reminders of the departed, like the first pressing of *The Joshua Tree* peeking out from my record collection.

That day when I encountered the monk, I began to speculate about a different life unfolding. I began to think of Oscar as motivated by human desire. I wanted him to run in the field like a gift I imagined my father had sent me. I wanted the cattle to react to Oscar's 'eye'. We completed the loop together on my father's anniversary and the trauma that I believed had once made Oscar run off in the early weeks of his arrival had gone. We had come full circle. The fields surrounding my home, the green Glenstal pastures, glistened as a field of dreams. And the dog I imagined Oscar had once been, caught in the 'time before', was the dog he always would be: a spirit of the wind tirelessly working to mend two hearts as one.

I had intended to end on this note, as one cycle of life completes a full circle, as if being was neat and tidy, and to have calmly walked past the fields of grazing cattle meant it was over: we had won. But life went on. And as time passed, habits and walks became daily rituals while Oscar was still changing – although not ever, I suspected, into the cattle-herding sheepdog of my vision at Glenstal. I often returned to that dream and its importance to the onwards turning cycle of existence: to the rescue; to the thoughts about the countryside; to the healing and nurturing properties of nature; to the freakouts when I thought he was lost; to the time he first hopped into his basket; to the mornings when he was so pent up to go outside, as if he had held in a wee for hours, but when the door opened he just froze and stared up at me. 'I'm going nowhere unless you are with me' were words I imagined contained within him. Or when I held him close in the back of the car, on a cold winter night, sometimes crying, sometimes laughing, sometimes on the phone, sometimes just thinking. Or on Keeper Hill in the Silvermines or on Moylussa in East Clare, approaching the difficult part near the top where the hike gets slippery and rocky and I wondered if Oscar would fall on the rocks. And then I watched as he made his way around a path that was difficult to even notice in the sun. *Oh that famed collie intelligence*, I thought to myself.

Our companionship matured on those hikes, though I still fixated on the dream vision at Glenstal: the one I posited as bringing our journey full circle. As 2020 passed into 2021 and on to 2022 and further on, and as Oscar maintained his youthful looks, time seemed to stand still in his presence and yet I remained fixated on the vision. I thought about it as some post-fix form of Irish mythology, like when a poet, caught in a dream state, confronts a beautiful woman who is later revealed to be a cipher for Ireland. The poems that contribute to this tradition – aislings – also evolved during Ireland's years of colonial oppression. In them, the beautiful woman appears to the forlorn poet as an object of desire – desire otherwise known as freedom. She enables the poet to dream of better days, to persist through hardship. Like my vision, the aisling took form as a dream, the poetic vehicle of choice when facing difficulty. It is a form that has seeped into every corner and crevice of

Ireland, from Murroe to Roundstone, from Ennsicrone to Killaloe, from Dublin to Kinsale. It has manifested as an unaccompanied song poem, when the otherworld is believed to enter the sinews and fibres of the singer poet, so that life itself becomes a celebration of our world and the next interchanging as one: the sonorous call of Ireland in both myth and reason.

By 2023, after several rounds of dry-needle therapy for my ailing knees, I began running again with Oscar, this time along the banks of the River Shannon, beside the University of Limerick – a river so infamous in Irish mythology, so rich in significance to the island. I thought more and more about the Glenstal vision as an aisling. Along the river, Oscar ran free, rarely leaving my side. I turned to see where he was as his ears flopped in the wind, his body rocking back and forward like a ship, while luxuriating in nature's bosom. Occasionally, he ran on ahead and I observed as he sat monk-like in the long grass, guarding the inlet beside the trees where walkers and their dogs would creep on through. He hunched there alone, his job to care for others like he watches over me.

Perhaps Oscar came to me as a vision, herding the cattle on the green pastures of Glenstal, like the woman in the aisling who represents all that is beautiful and seductive about her island but not necessarily true, in the strictest sense of the word. Maybe he too is a portal into my imagination, renewing my own vision of Ireland. He is a lure into the landscape, a coileán helping in his own way. A sheepdog named Oscar invigorating our life, through the simple act of being with me.

The aisling tradition is mirrored in indigenous rituals across the world. Dreamtime takes form as songlines and walkways littering the land, not unlike those I shaped as part of my walks with Oscar as we hiked the landscape. The Clare Glens, Slieve Felim, Keeper Hill, Moylussa, Knockma, Knocknarea and then, in more recent times, the Shannon banks – the river that delineates the western province from which I hail. For the Irish mystic philosopher John Moriarty, dreamtime is an awakening, to the mythos intricately tied to place. It is poetic activity that has to be re-energised, renewed over time, given new form as language knits itself into the materiality of other worlds. As I ran the banks of the Shannon with Oscar, waving at the walkers who had become part of our community since 2020, new songlines were forged from imagining the Oscar I envisaged manoeuvring the Glenstal herd with ease, not as some pretend reality, but as part of Moriarty's aisling tradition, when reformulated as a contemporary concern.

A sheepdog named *Oscar*. I had assumed his name was a nod to a beloved Irish poet, Oscar Wilde. It was a name I had never dwelled on, thinking it derived from the same Anglo-Irish tradition as Wilde. In the early months of his adoption, I jokingly referred to Oscar as 'Oscar Wild' and the picture I took of him in those initial days is still one cherished to this day. In the photograph, he wades through the grass fields behind our house, exuberantly pulling Anton along with him at a time when we still lacked the confidence to let him run free in the lush pastures. This same photograph, from way back, is how I will always remember him, dragging us, as a family, into the future, through fields that twist and turn to make a home, dragging us forward when our feet are stuck in the past. His smile, his coat just fresh from the groomer, his elegance, his attentiveness, his stoic nervousness: his love. His mythos, his Irishness, his shape and his intelligence. His being there.

I stood on the banks of the Shannon, fixating on dreamtime (in Moriarty's use of the word) and all its attendant exoticism. I thought of vision as an awakening to place and a forging of myth. Then I circled back to the name again. *Oscar.* For the duration of our time together, through all our escapades and years in tandem, the walks when he ran on ahead only to circle back, spherical movement that settled into a mantra, I had never dwelt on the name as meaning anything more than that of a dog who made his way into my life. Oscar was his name. That was all I needed to know. That was it.

That day on the Shannon, I returned to the car and opened the boot for Oscar to jump in, leaping like Faugheen the champion racehorse. He nestled into the corner of the boot and stared up at me with his gentle eyes. Then I googled 'Oscar and Irish myth', interchanging with 'Celtic myth', and a stream of information poured onto the screen from multiple sources. In the eight years since Oscar entered my life, I had not done this. It was telling, almost inexplicable. I think I knew in the recesses of my brain that Oscar was the mythic son of Oisín and grandson of Ireland's most infamous mythic hero Fionn Mac Cumhaill. The story of Fionn and 'the Fianna' as heroic Irish warriors defending the country in the pre-Christian age is recorded across Ireland and the Celtic nations from many orally transmitted sources with minor differences in its detail. I was told these stories as a child by

my father. These tales found a new level of popularity across Europe in the eighteenth century when the Scottish highlander poet James Macpherson published his *Ossian* poems, retelling the story of the Fianna through the lens of Scots Gaelic. Although Macpherson's Fingal is practically identical to the mythic hero of Irish lore, as told across Ireland, the origin of the poem is still disputed.

Oscar is my dog's name. But mythic Oscar is the grandson of Fionn in Irish lore. He is also a renowned warrior whose death gives rise to the only explicit show of emotion by Fionn in the entire mythic cycle. Fionn cries when he hears that his grandson, considered goofy and awkward (before he emerges as the hero many critics believe personifies the heart of Ireland), has died from wounds accrued in battle. Two stories are of major importance to Oscar's growing status across the world, derived from Gaelic culture. The first is 'Bruidhean Chaorthainn', translated as 'Hostel of the Quicken Trees'. In this story, Erin (Ireland) is attacked by King Colgán of Lochlainn, killing key members of the famed Fianna. Oscar settles the affairs in a ferocious battle with Colgán. Solidifying his notoriety as a brave avenger, the story is significant in that Colgán's son Midrac is spared and allowed to live his life on an island on the River Shannon. It is on the matching Shannon banks I run with Oscar, the same place that I began to make all these associations that stem from a name. The mythic action continued on the Shannon with the Fianna again the point of attack. This time, Sinsar, reigning king of the world during that period, is the main enemy. For a second time, Oscar defends the island of Erin, infamously beheading his attacker in an act of vengeance.

Oscar is a mythical name, a name that travelled from Ireland to Scotland on the same route, some believe, as the 'coileán' in Britain's border counties, emerging as the 'collie' helper – a dog that helps, just like the mythical Oscar who helped the Fianna to survive. A sheepdog named Oscar – whose namesake is regaled across Ireland as *the* mythic warrior, whose explicit bravery and loyalty, dying from a fatal wound in battle – is celebrated in the second story 'Cath Gahbra'.

'Oscar' became widespread in the nineteenth century in the cultural afterlife of Macpherson's poetry, the epic published in the shadow of the Romantic movement across Ireland, Scotland and Wales. The name soon spread further afield as the character of Oscar became known as the one who stands 'unrivalled and alone' in translations. Mythic Oscar is far from perfect; he falls asleep and loses concentration on the job. But he is also the most effectively human, perhaps even the most likeable, of fable heroes in the Fianna cycle. 'O, Oscar! bend the strong in arms; but spare the feeble hand. Be thou a stream of mighty tides against the foes of thy people; but like the gale that moves the grass to those who ask thine aid,' Macpherson writes in praise of him.

Oscar Fingal O'Flahertie Wills Wilde was born in Dublin, a literary star whose life also takes the form of modern myth, courageously recalibrating Victorian mores around his sexual identity. In the late twentieth century, the English pop star of major Irish extraction, Steven Patrick Morrissey, sang with panache, infamously declaring on 'Cemetry Gates' (taken from the seminal Smiths' album, *The Queen is Dead*), that 'Keats and Yeats are on your side, but you lose, because weird lover Wilde is on mine.' In my teens, these lyrics were a rally cry for those afraid, those with few songlines to map their own identity.

The imprisoned Oscar Wilde stood up to his gaolers with courage and bravery. The name travelled further to Germany. Oskar Schindler was a businessman who faced down Nazi bluster and propaganda to save many lives, becoming the subject of Thomas Keneally's bestselling novel, *Schindler's Ark* and adapted by Steven Spielberg into his Oscar-winning film *Schindler's List*. And today there is the sheepdog Oscar, who ran along the songline of Glenstal in the summer of 2020 with his friend and handler, a scholar and perhaps even a writer. He ran with this same handler for many years, helping him move into the future, to touch base with his imagination so that the landscape became part of his own mythology of the present.

A monk was standing in their way, but the writer was too distracted, caught in the reverie he would later compose as an opening to rootedness and place: an aisling. He – that is *I* – would tell a story about befriending a sheepdog named Oscar, long before this moment of reverie, this distillation of dream and vision, captured the moment. As I ventured through Glenstal on my father's anniversary, re-realising the landscape, I was turning it into a place called home. But it was not until years later that I would connect this to a name; that the name Oscar jumped out at me when running the banks of the Shannon with my dog beside me, an Oscar I had come to love immensely. I fell into the misty banks of time and myth, yet the past was no longer my unwanted inheritance.

My father was whispering stories of the Fianna into my ear as I fell asleep in his presence, with past and present swimming together as one.

The Shannon faded in the distance that day as the car made its way home towards Murroe. Keeper Hill stood out in front, the clouds gathering on its peak and the rare sun assembling its force. The Slieve Felim mountains had their little pathways leading up to the peak. The mountains of Ébliu, named after the ancient goddess, meaning beauty and radiance, have since become known as Felim. A sheepdog's head was placed on the armrest between the seats at the front as new songlines took shape all around, glowing on a fresh green landscape. As these lines took their final form in front of me, my father's words were still whistling in my ear. The landscape I was led to after his death, the place a sheepdog named Oscar had made his way to me many years prior, appeared all around, as though unearthly light was shining down on me. These were like lights made up of new lines emblazoned on an old land: a revised Ireland still somehow the same as the old and ancient earth. On this land, a helper had come to me as a dream, bringing the promise of better days.

Epilogue:
Twisting and Turning
into a New Day

I think it was the August Bank Holiday of 2019, the biggest summer holiday weekend in Ireland, but it is difficult to recall the exact date because it is near-mythic as an event and is hard to distinguish as real. Anton was staying with a friend in Kilkee, a small village in West Clare close to the Cliffs of Moher, probably the most visited natural landmark on the Wild Atlantic Way, a route that traverses Ireland's west coast from Cork to Donegal. On the Monday that Anton was due to come home, it was sunny and mild, perfect for a picnic and a day at the beach. We took the decision to collect him as a family, to make a day out of it – to drench in Ireland's sun! The car was packed in haste, togs added in the hope of stopping on the coast for a swim. Oscar would come along too.

In summer, a cohort of Limerick city dwellers decant to the villages of Kilkee and Lahinch, on the west coast of Clare, a region within Munster that's a haven of natural beauty. From the long cliff walks in and around Loop Head to the unique limestone calcification of the Burren region, famous for its sparse landscape, the coastline is awash with culture, mythology, music and tourism. It is packed with young people on the August weekend, as Limerick's youth hit the coast in droves.

For more than two years, I had tried to coax Oscar into water of some sort. I sometimes stopped at the stream beside the wood near our house after heavy rain helped fashion a hefty little pull in the current. I would try to entice Oscar in as I bundled through the water in wellingtons, but he was terrified. He just stood there, hesitant and scared, before backing off. His stand-off reminded me of when I was young, watching my father hurl our Jack Russells into water to relieve them of their fear, willingly or not. He did this so they would swim the 'doggy paddle' instinctually. Of course, if they were in bother he would jump in and help them back to safety. But I didn't have it in me to hurl Oscar in. I tried again during a swim in Enniscrone when the waves crashed in upon the shore and the white foam engulfed my body momentarily. Still, he would not take the plunge with me. He would wander in a little, allowing the water to submerge his paws, before backing off. After he began to bark, his sound effects were added as he frantically patrolled the beach, never taking his eye off me while I jumped up and down in the waves.

On another occasion, at the Clare Glens, an otter – or possibly even a mink – ran out in front of us on our walk (minks are an invasive species that have a detrimental impact on Irish wildlife). Oscar was so furious at the creature's lack of decorum that he sprinted with all his might into the bushes after it, along a steep decline towards the waterfall. Unable to see his whereabouts, I grew frantic with worry that he might slip into the water and be carried downstream. But it was soon apparent that he hadn't slipped. His delicate balance had helped him to peer into the abyss, before slowly edging his way back to me. Another disaster averted.

En route to Kilkee that August morning, we took the inland road from Ennis, through the villages of Kilmihill and Cooraclare, before arriving at Kilrush, only a short distance from Kilkee. As we drove through Kilrush, a small inlet appeared where people were walking down with beach materials in hand: wind breakers, picnic baskets etc. I suggested to Ylva that it might be quieter to stop at this beach for an hour before collecting Anton. Kilkee beach would be mobbed.

She agreed and we parked near the water before making our way down to the side of the beach. It was a busy spot but not overcrowded. Lots of people were gathered there; some picnicking, some applying sun cream, all engaging in the usual beach activities. The day was getting hotter with every passing minute and the shallow, almost static water stood out as the perfect remedy. We stopped at a rock to sit for some time, Oscar held on a lead. We were there twenty minutes when Ylva and Karl decided to go back to the car for something. I slipped off my shoes and let Oscar off so he could stand at the shore and watch me as I took a cool dip. It was only on entering the water that the difficulty of actually swimming became apparent to me. As I slid into the water, the shallowness seemed to extend for ever.

Usually in the Atlantic, the water deepens sharply, so that a swimmer can dive in from a standing position a few yards into the sea. But when I entered the water at Kilrush, the shallow shelving went on and on. I had to push further out until the beach of people appeared like a mash of dots from afar. I must have waded in 150 yards. I remember thinking it was the shallowest tide I had encountered and it took far too much effort to make it out to where the first swimmer bobbed. And then I was in, letting the water embrace me, my fingers moving ever so slightly through it.

More bobbing heads surfaced on the water, as my eyes squinted until I found I was surrounded by men, women and children. The midday sun was brushing the surface of the water, making it difficult to distinguish one face from another. I soon became disoriented, unsure as to where the water deepened. It was a strange and discomforting experience, unlike the sea I had spent my life swimming in.

There is a song about the impulse to swim by the band Songs: Ohia called 'Lioness'. It is written, like all their songs, by their mercurial frontman Jason Molina. The lyrics tell the story of a lion and lioness who are separated by the River Nile. It is a simple story about the love the lioness feels for the object of her desire across the river. The crux of the story is that she risks her life to make it across. 'Whether you save me, whether you savage me,' Molina sings in a tender voice, 'I want my last look to be the moon in your eyes, want my heart to break if it must break in your jaws.' This final part of the song depicts the contradictions of love, its dangerous capacity to intoxicate and hypnotise, with the refrain touching on life's basest emotions. Molina then repeats the line 'If you can't get here fast enough' over and over until it starts to grate, releasing the most powerful recant after 'I will swim to you'. The same line is repeated five or so times, invested with a burning passion. Some days I listened to the song on repeat, waiting each time for that killer line to affect me, the display of love so beautifully stated.

I lifted my head up from the water at Kilrush to find a disgruntled expression awaiting me. 'Get him out. He's filthy. Dogs aren't allowed to swim in the estuary.' The comment was practically hurled into my face. I turned in the direction of the shore, sunlight creating silver flashes on the water. Along the surface, I saw a black-and-white coloured head, a white line down the front of its nose, pushing through the water towards me. I realised it was Oscar, with his feet pedalling like a devil through the water, his face breaking out into a smile. As he approached, he began to circle around me. It was one of the most incredible and moving sights I have encountered, as if the heavens had opened. 'Get him out!' the man shouted. In a huff, I replied that Oscar was cleaner than most humans. I grabbed Oscar's feet, feeling his wet coat in my arms and tried to shuttle him back to the shore. He was heavy to carry. So I just let him swim as we powered back together, Oscar pushing behind me. We swam as one until I could stand. Then I lifted him onto the beach, to where Ylva and Karl waited, watching.

I still struggle to distinguish the emotions that overwhelmed my senses in the estuary that day. Pride? Perhaps, like the pride in a child who takes its first step. Or shock? Shock Oscar did something so unexpected, so laden with meaning. He had swum to me. Something had rattled him into action, a head moving further and further away, like a feather blowing in the wind. Maybe it was love – the love for a companion that makes us lose ourselves in the moment.

I'll never know because a bark is not speech and Oscar cannot tell me. But I can surmise. And I did so, as the name Oscar swirled in my consciousness. *Oscar*: the ferocious and fearless warrior.

It was a name that spread from Ireland to Europe and on to the Americas, Australia and New Zealand, and further again. We stood at the estuary where the Shannon meets the Atlantic, a point where one entity merges into another. It was the location where myth meets reality. For the River Shannon derives its names from the myth of Sionnan, the same mythical goddess who drowned in a flooded well; the river was named in the heroine's honour. Sionnan was thought to possess such great wisdom. Oscar, named after a warrior who travelled the Shannon banks, swam through the estuary to be with me.

On the drive home later that day, bypassing Ennis on our way to the motorway, Oscar sat in the back, his head sticking up from behind. I gazed to one side at the east, towards where he was found in Kilkishen, reaching over the hills to Lough Derg, its colour scheme so unique to the region. On my right, to the other side, the River Shannon estuary passed down along the west of the county to where we had just come from, swirling in and out of time, making its way to a coast that would eventually lead to the Americas; a shore littered with sea stacks and cliffs, and home to whales, dolphins, basking sharks and puffins.

Now, from a 2025 vantage point called the present, that day when Oscar and I ran along the Shannon banks reflecting on a name, as a new mythology weaved into the landscape, retains a crystal clarity. So too that day thought to be in 2019, when we travelled home along a motorway; a family returning from Kilrush. The sun shone down and the wind flittered in the window, yet the driver's thoughts were elsewhere: his mind busy picturing a dog's legs pulsing through the water, like something from another world; a dog's legs twisting and turning along the wheels of time into a new instant − a day that may or may not be better than the last.

Works Cited

Opening epigraphs

James Macpherson, *Fragments of Ancient Poetry* (1760).

Augustine of Hippo, *Homilies on the First Epistle of John* (New York: New City Press, 2008).

Benedict Anderson, *Imagined Communities: Reflections on the Origins and Spread of Nationalism* (London: Verso, 2016).

Chantal Akerman, trans. Daniella Shreir, *My Mother Laughs* (London: Silver Press, 2019).

Augustine of Hippo, *Homilies on the First Epistle of John* (New York: New City Press, 2008).

Dante Aligheri, trans. Henry Wadsworth Longfellow, *Inferno*, edited and preface by Matthew Pearl (London: Modern Library, 2003).

Eileen Battersby, *Ordinary Dogs* (London: Faber & Faber, 2013).

Sue Donaldson and Will Kymlicka, *Zoopolis: A Political Theory of Animal Rights* (Oxford: Oxford University Press, 2013).

Bob Dylan, *Blood on the Tracks*, Columbia Records, 1975.

Carol Gilligan, *In a Different Voice: Psychological Theory and Women's Development* (Cambridge: Harvard University Press, 2016).

Donna J. Haraway, *The Companion Species Manifesto: Dogs, People, and Significant Otherness* (Chicago: University of Chicago Press, 2003).

Thomas Keneally, *Schindler's Ark* (London: Hodder & Stoughton, 1982).

The Wind Will Carry Us, dir. Abbas Kiarostami, New Yorker Films, MK2 Productions, 1999.

sleep furiously, dir. Gideon Koppel, Bard Entertainment/Van Film, 2008.

Helen Macdonald, *H is for Hawk* (London: Vintage, 2015).

James Macpherson, ed. Howard Gaskill, *The Poems of Ossian and Related Works* (Edinburgh: Edinburgh University Press, 2020).

Donald McCaig, *Nop's Trials: A Novel* (New York: Crown Publishers, Inc, 1984).

John Moriarty, *Dreamtime* (Dublin: Lilliput Press, 1994).

Sarah Perry, 'Drive Your Plow Over the Bones of the Dead by Olga Tokarczuk – the entire cosmic catastrophe', *Guardian*, 21 September 2018.

Denise Riley, *Say Something Back* (London: Picador, 2016).

Denise Riley, *Time Lived, Without Its Flow* (London: Picador, 2019).

Withnail and I, dir. Bruce Robinson, Arrow Films, 1987.

Mark Rowlands, *The Philosopher and the Wolf: Lessons from the Wild on Love, Death and Happiness* (London: Granta Books, 2008).

Jonathan Safran Foer, *Eating Animals* (London: Penguin, 2010).

Roger Scruton, *On Hunting* (London: Yellow Jersey, 1998).

Rupert Sheldrake, *Dogs That Know When Their Owners Are*

Coming Home: The Unexplained Powers of Animals (London: Penguin, 2000).

Peter Singer, *Animal Liberation* (London: Bodley Head, 2015).

The Smiths, *The Queen is Dead*, Rough Trade Records, 1986.

Songs: Ohia, *The Lioness*, Secretly Canadian, 2000.

Schindler's List, dir. Steven Spielberg, Amblin Entertainment & Universal Pictures, 1993.

Finding Nemo, dir. Andrew Stanton, Pixar/Disney, 2003.

Mirror, dir. Andrei Tarkovsky, Mosfilm, 1975.

Olga Tokarczuk, trans. Antonia Lloyd-Jones, *Drive Your Plow Over the Bones of the Dead* (London: Fitzcarraldo Editions, 2019).

U2, *The Joshua Tree*, Island Records, 1987.

U2, *The Joshua Tree (Remastered)*, Universal Island Records under licence to Mercury Records, 2007.

The Waterboys, *Fisherman's Blues*, Ensign Records, 1988.

Kanye West, *The Life of Pablo*, GOOD/Def Jam Records, 2016.

Neil Young, *On the Beach*, Reprise Records, 1974.

Acknowledgements

There are so many contributors to Team Oscar that I want to shout out to. Carrie Paterson at DoppelHouse Press in the US has been the project's foremost supporter. Her faith in the undertaking when it was seemingly on the back foot has been a big part of its success. The editorial team at Simon & Schuster UK, especially Kris Doyle, Kat Ailes and production editor Florence Garnett, have been fantastic and professional at all times. Thanks also to Nige Tassell for the forensic copy edit and the collie solidarity. Thanks to Liane Payne for illustrating, with such exquisite detail, the book's key landmarks. Much appreciation to Laurie McShea and Hannah Paget at S&S UK marketing and publicity, and to their Irish counterparts Declan Heeney and Simon Hess at Gill Hess, Dublin. My agent, Marianne Gunn O'Connor, has been an immeasurable support and I am incredibly grateful to her. Thanks to Donal Ryan for putting us in touch at a trying time.

Oscar never would have come into my life but for two seemingly innocuous conversations: one was with Loe McDonagh, the other with Anne Stewart. Loe told me sheepdogs are great, if not the greatest of companions, and Anne brought me to one – if not the best. Thank you so much.

I am grateful to Peter Delpeut, Mickey Gorman and Aryan Kaganof for all the initial support: you are true artists. During the early editing process, I was grieving the loss of my friend Robert Purcell who died tragically in 2023. I am grateful to Robert for his camaraderie, empathy and love. I travelled across Tasmania with another friend, Grant Nolan, as the US edition of *A Sheepdog Named Oscar* entered its initial stages; I offer particular thanks to Grant for his support at that difficult time and throughout our lifetime. Thanks are given to Michael Vallely for his ongoing friendship and assistance, and for all the stellar work done on the North American edition of the audiobook. And to my other Tuam friends: Paul Fleming, Joe McBreen, John Hoban, Tommy Keane, Conor O'Dea and Jamie Ralph, and those who rallied after Purce's death. And to my sadly deceased childhood pal Jarlath 'Ja' Keane, who set me on the music path, the influence of which flickers through here.

My father Dr John A. Waldron and grandfather Dr Tony Waldron are significant influences on the memoir throughout. The west of Ireland has inspired the stories given form in the book and the Waldron family instilled a great love of the tales from the old mythical Ireland into its present.

Davey (David) and Bridie (Bridget) Rainsford, Tom Holmes, Mike Ryan (RIP) – neighbours who show up in the book – welcomed our family to Murroe and I am exceptionally grateful to them. Gratitude extends to those who read drafts of the book, offering measured feedback in return: Ger Lane,

Céline Linssen, Becky Watson, Tom Inglis, Tommy Bonner, Fr Anthony Keane, Frank Armstrong, Louise Purcell, Michael Holly, Kamila Kuc, Gideon Koppel and Damien O'Connell.

My colleagues at LSAD have been exceedingly supportive at all times. I want to thank my deans Mike Fitzpatrick and Anthony Caleshu, in addition to Louise Masterson, Susan Halvey, Lorraine Neeson, Alan Keane, Katrina Maguire, Ciara Healy and Cormac Morrison. A special, overdue thank you to LSAD's East Clare admin division, Jill Lees and Muriel Dinneen, for many years of quiet and unyielding support. There are many friends whose considered input, in no short measure, I also want to acknowledge: Brian Fenton, Michael G. Kelly, Declan Flanagan and Lyndsey Clarke, Johnny McWeeney, Martin Walsh, Maggie Mikaitis, Micheál and Caroline O'hAodha, Jack Anderson, Niall and Padraig Fahy, David Whelan, John Ryan, Karl O'Sullivan, Jonathan Quinn, Mark Moran, Fergal Cox, Mark McGrane, James Lee, Mark O'Byrne, Mat Rappaport, Ted Hardin and Elizabeth Coffman, Don Farrell and Susan Dargan, Brian and Eileen Coates, Joakim and Anna Larsson, and Frances McCartan. Sincere thanks to Mary Gunning for permission to visit and photograph the farm Oscar had lived on.

Also: a shout-out to Abbey Boarding Kennels, Ella's Boarding Kennels, A Round of A Paws and Mulcair Vets (Newport), who cared for Oscar over the years. To MADRA for their tireless dedication to rescuing and rehabilitating Irish sheepdogs. And to Laura Dillon, the good neighbour and vet nurse who fed and cared for Oscar when he lived alone on the farm.

My family are spread across these pages on the journey with me. My wife Ylva, the apple of Oscar's eye, has shown such care and patient love encouraging me in everything I do. Thank you for everything. Our boys Anton and Karl have lit the way. My mother Mary is always there; through fog and rain, the thick and thin. My sisters Sheila and Kate offer ongoing encouragement, as does my extended family in both Ireland and Sweden: Alberto Blanco, Eva Holmgren, Kerstin Holmgren, Malin Holmgren, Göran Hedström, Conal Lowry and Sue Dermody, Tony Lowry, Peter Lowry and Ciara O'Donnell. Thanks to my late Uncle Tim McFadden for the stories, the craic and inspiration. To family and friends not mentioned above, who gave much needed support, I am incredibly grateful. A major nod to Janey Mac, Oscar's border collie sis, for spicing up his life while bringing calm, in addition to the Shannon Banks dog-walking community who made us part of their life (a special shout out to Gracie! And Bonnie, in memoriam). And to the sheepdog named Oscar – who appeared when I needed him, becoming the glue sticking us together under the shadow my father's death – I thank you from the bottom of my heart. Finally, but no less significantly, I dedicate this book to my son Anton Waldron, for the love that always shines through the Irish rain, and for the courage and resilience shown in the most testing times.